MARKETING
IN A
NUTSHELL

About the author

Sheri Bridges is an associate professor of marketing in the School of Business at Wake
Forest University. In the 20 years since she graduated from Stanford University with a Ph.D.
in marketing, she has taught courses in marketing, consumer behavior, brand management,
new product development, integrated marketing communications and marketing strategy to
undergraduate, full-time MBA, evening MBA and executive MBA students.

Printed in the United States of America

ISBN 978-0-9834157-2-5

Table of Contents

Preface

Ask faculty (this author included!) what comes to mind when they hear the word "textbooks" and more than a few will reply: Thick, heavy, overpriced, boring encyclopedias full of endless lists, definitions and details that most practitioners don't use . . . or even know. In addition to such an unflattering description, they might complain that irrelevant information often is included at the expense of critical topics at the very heart of a discipline – topics that, if they're addressed at all, are given only superficial coverage.

Many students (including you, perhaps?) would likely respond with a similar description, adding their own lament: "If the instructor isn't going to lecture from or discuss the book in class, why should I spend my money to buy it and my time to read it?" (An August 2011 survey by the U.S. Public Interest Research Group, a nonprofit consumer-advocacy organization, revealed that seven in 10 college students had declined to purchase a textbook at least once because they thought the price was too high.)

MARKETING IN A NUTSHELL is designed to address these criticisms by eliminating content extraneous to an introductory course and giving you the essentials of a basic marketing education. It covers the concepts that are fundamental to marketing theory and practice and that all business students, regardless of major, should know and understand.

Traditional introductory textbooks typically begin with an overview of marketing, including the comprehensive (if turgid and long-winded!) definition developed by the American Marketing Association (". . . the activity, set of institutions, and processes for creating, communicating, delivering, and exchanging offerings that have value for customers, clients, partners, and society at large"); a description of the components of marketing (the four Ps: product/service, price, place and promotion); a history of the discipline (production focus, sales era, market orientation and, finally, the focus on value creation); and a delineation of the requirements for marketing to occur (two or more parties with unsatisfied needs, a desire and ability to satisfy those needs, a way for the parties to communicate, and something to exchange).

MARKETING IN A NUTSHELL omits much of that material (beyond what's above, of course!), instead opening with a specification of the basic objective of most businesses and a description of how marketing helps achieve that objective. This "beginning at the very beginning" approach reveals marketing's true position in an organization – *as an indispensible, primal ingredient of a firm's day-to-day operations and long-term success,* not *optional icing on its competitive strategy.*

If this is your first encounter with marketing in a classroom, as opposed to as a consumer, the best way to think about the book's concepts might be to relate them to companies, brands, ads, retailers, trends or situations with which you're familiar. For example, the next chapter introduces the four Ps. What strategy does your favorite brand employ for each of the variables and why? The *what* question requires you to *know* something about the brand; the *why* question requires you to *think* about the reason behind the what. *Knowing is important, but thinking is crucial.*

Because **MARKETING IN A NUTSHELL** is so concise, reading assignments won't take you as long to complete as they would with a conventional textbook. Consequently, you'll have more opportunity to think about the material and how it applies to the businesses and brands you know.

Class time will be used to deepen your understanding of critical concepts and enhance your ability to identify, analyze and solve marketing-related problems. The more you think about the material before you arrive, the more meaningful – and enjoyable – each session will be for you.

Here's a question to help get your brain in gear:

CNBC once interviewed Indra Nooyi, CEO of PepsiCo, which owns Frito-Lay, and Warren Buffett, CEO of Berkshire Hathaway, a diversified holding company whose subsidiaries include GEICO, Dairy Queen, Fruit of the Loom, and Benjamin Moore, among many others. Buffett, who is Coca-Cola's largest shareholder, was asked why he doesn't also hold stock in PepsiCo.

"It – Pepsi – it's a wonderful company. And particularly, I mean, Frito-Lay is a fabulous business. I'd love to own it. I eat Fritos, I eat Cheetos, I eat their potato chips; I even eat Munchos, which are kind of hard to find. But I always drink Coca-Cola with them," he replied.

Researchers associated with the Human Neuroimaging Lab at Baylor College of Medicine conducted blind taste tests with subjects who sampled Coke and Pepsi while their brain activity was monitored. When asked which unnamed, unlabeled soda they preferred, about half said Coke and the other half Pepsi. However, blood flow to the brain's reward center was five times stronger when participants drank Pepsi than when they drank Coke.

After subjects were told which of the two samples was Coke, the number of people who said they favored that brand's taste increased to 75 percent. Moreover, once the Coke had been identified, blood flow to areas of the brain associated with drinkers' thinking and judging activities increased http://www.cell.com/neuron/abstract/S0896-6273(04)00612-9.

Given that blind taste tests consistently show balance between liking for the two cola brands, why do you think more people claim to prefer Coke?

What does Coke have that Pepsi doesn't?

Chapter 1: Marketing and its role in business

Welcome to marketing, the discipline that keeps businesses in business!

Maybe you hadn't considered marketing in those terms, but when you do stop and think about it, it makes sense. After all, you know that companies need money to operate, and that they get money by selling things to customers. You know all about customers because, like billions of other individuals and organizations around the world, you are one. You know that marketing is about finding and keeping customers because you've seen thousands of television commercials, product packages, billboards, coupons, magazine ads, store salespeople, Internet pop-ups, and subway posters persuading you – or someone you know – to buy, buy now, buy here, buy this and not that, buy more and buy more often.

No organization of any kind – a not-for-profit, a charity, a for-profit, a corporation, a partnership, a limited liability company – can stay in existence without customers, unless it's a government entity funded by tax revenues.

Customers can be art patrons who bequeath money to museums; citizens who donate canned goods to shelters; voters who contribute to political parties; clients who patronize hair salons; corporations who buy raw materials from other corporations; patients who visit physicians; shoppers who purchase from online retailers; audiences who watch TV programs; spectators who attend sporting events . . . .

You get the picture. Organizations need customers to support what they do. For some, the support they require isn't financial. For most, however, it is.

The purpose of a for-profit business

Although the marketing concepts described in this manual are important for all organizations, regardless of their type, the next two sections pertain specifically to for-profit companies. For-profits exist for the specific purpose of making money. Or, rather, *earning* money from their customers.

Earning money *from* customers *for* whom?

** The fundamental purpose of a for-profit firm is to maximize the value created for shareholders, who are its *owners*. **

Entrepreneurs start for-profit businesses and shareholders buy stock in for-profit companies because they expect positive returns on their investments. Individuals who purchase shares in existing companies hope the shares, which grant them ownership status, will either pay regular dividends or will appreciate in price so they can someday be sold at a gain. Entrepreneurs and shareholders/owners count on receiving economic value from for-profit firms.

If you choose to work for a for-profit organization after you graduate, it will be important for you to realize that although you might work under the supervision of a particular manager or vice-president, you will actually be working *for*, or on behalf of, the shareholders who own the company. The decisions you make and the actions you take should be designed to protect the interests of the owners by preserving and protecting the firm's future cash flows, which depend on offering the right product/service, targeting the right customer, and *always always always* doing the right (i.e., ethical) thing.

Why the sudden focus on owners? If organizations can't exist without customers, what about them? What about employees? And retailers? And suppliers? And support service providers? And the community in which the firm is located? And the people who live in the areas in which the firm operates?

We'll get to those. For right now, however, let's take this concept of maximizing owner value down to its simplest level by using an example to which many of us can relate.

Suppose when you were 10 years old you opened a lemonade stand to earn money to purchase a Burton Whammy Bar Snowboard. You borrowed $25 from your parents to buy sugar, lemons, cups, bags of ice, napkins and signboards. Using a table and chair from your bedroom, you set up your stand on Saturday mornings from 9 o'clock till 11 o'clock, even on those days when you wanted to stay in bed or when it was so hot the ice melted or when all your friends were outside playing.

Because your lemonade was much tastier than that sold by other stands in the neighborhood and because you picked a great corner location, you had loads of customers. The steady flow of customers meant a steady flow of cash. After just three Saturdays you had enough money to pay back your parents, cover the cost of more ingredients to make more lemonade to sell to more people, and almost fill your piggybank.

You were creating value for customers by quenching their thirst, and customers were creating value for you by purchasing your lemonade. You figured that by the end of the summer, you'd be able to buy the snowboard, some new clothes, and maybe an MP3 player.

You worked hard; you earned money from customers who preferred your lemonade or your service or your location – or all three – to the competition's. *The cash was yours to save or spend because you owned the "company."*

Capitalism: a business philosophy

Owners are very important under *capitalism*, which is the economic foundation of business in the United States. Owners of firms invest funds that they could have used in other ways, and they always face the risk of losing their money if the companies fail. They're willing to take risks because they expect to be rewarded for doing so in the form of profits. The creation of valuable offerings for customers, such as your lemonade, is one of the most important keys to profitability. If no one bought your product, you eventually would be forced to shut down your stand and you would lose the $25 you invested in supplies.

According to a 2010 report issued by the U.S. Small Business Administration, firms with fewer than 500 employees accounted for 64 percent of the 22.5 million net new jobs between 1993 and 2008. Such firms employ more than half of all private sector workers and represent 44 percent of the country's total private payroll (http://www.sba.gov/sites/default/files/files/an%20analysis%20of%20small%20business%20 and%20jobs(1).pdf). Clearly, entrepreneurs and shareholders – capitalists who are willing to invest in new and ongoing businesses – are critical to a growing economy.

Of course, local, state and federal governments also have roles. In the U.S., government is chiefly responsible for defense, roads, the justice system and education. It also regulates private industry and provides welfare, unemployment and other benefits to people in need. However, private enterprises produce most goods and services.

The tenets of capitalism are:

- Private ownership of the means by which goods and services are produced;
- Free markets in which:
    - companies compete for customers against other firms for their own economic gain;
    - production, distribution, and prices are affected by forces of supply and demand;
    - the primary role of government is protection of private property rights.

Even though your lemonade stand is a small business and many corporations are big businesses, you all share the same purpose: *creating value for the owner(s)*. The difference is that corporations have to consider other people and other factors as well. They must be concerned with the well-being of *all* their stakeholders, who are the people, groups, communities and systems that can affect and be affected by the corporation's activities and actions.

Why? For many possible reasons, but in particular because non-owning stakeholders can positively or negatively influence the corporation's ability to maximize owner value.

In addition to owners, stakeholders include customers, employees, suppliers, distributors, retailers, support service providers, creditors and communities. It's obvious that without customers, there are no sales and, therefore, no money coming into the company. And it's equally obvious that without employees, there's no one to produce the goods and services that customers would buy.

The roles of the other stakeholders might not be as obvious, but they're vital, too. Organizations need suppliers of raw materials used in the production of goods or services. Once goods or services have been produced, they need distributors and retailers to sell to customers. Support service providers, such as the insurance firm that covers employees; the trucking company that delivers finished products to retailers; the caterers who staff the employee cafeteria; and others, are all essential, too. So are the creditors, or financial institutions, that provide investment capital. And the community in which the organization is located is a source of human and other vital resources.

When a firm creates value for stakeholders, customers buy its goods or services, employees are productive, suppliers offer the best prices and terms of sale, retailers provide the most desirable shelf space – all of which create value for the firm and, consequently, for its owners.

Marketing and its role in business

Naturally, owners can't exist without companies to own. And, as previously noted, companies can't exist without customers to buy. Henry Ford put it well when he said, "It is not the employer who pays the wages. Employers only handle the money. It is the customer who pays the wages."

Consequently, because they're the source of the all-important cash flows that keep a business in business, customers have to be at the very heart of a company's mission.

** **Companies don't *make* money; customers give it to them.** **

All the functional areas of business are crucial to an organization's success. *Accounting* compiles and communicates financial information to internal and external decision makers. *Finance* acquires and allocates financial resources to maximize the economic value of the firm. *HR* manages human capital to create value for customers and other stakeholders. *MIS* collects, stores, analyzes and disseminates information for use in managerial decision-making. *Production/operations* transforms inputs into value-delivering customer outputs.

Marketing plays an especially critical role in the success of most firms for one very simple reason:

** Customers deliver dollars, and marketing delivers customers. **

Of course, marketing is not the only area involved in attracting and keeping customers. It is, however, the only one completely obsessed with them!

** Marketing is the process of creating, maintaining and improving mutually valuable customer relationships. **

Note the key words in this simple definition:

Process implies that marketing activities are continuous and without end.

Creating indicates that relationships with customers must be actively cultivated.

Maintaining suggests that customer relationships don't come with a lifetime loyalty guarantee.

Improving connotes the need to strengthen and enhance customer relationships over time.

Valuable captures the motivation for the relationship.

Mutually conveys the need for reciprocal benefits to the relationship.

Relationships implies that one customer is *not* as good as any other and that lasting connections, not one-time transactions, should be the marketer's goal.

Mutually valuable customer relationships are created, maintained and improved through the design and development of superior products/services *and* superior strategies for marketing them. A "bad" product – one of insufficient value to consumers – that's poorly marketed will obviously fail, as will a bad product that's marketed well and a good product that's poorly marketed.

| | Product/service | |
	Good	Bad
Good	Fabulous!	Fad
Bad	Fizzle	Flop!

Marketing strategy has four primary components, which are commonly referred to as the *four Ps: product, price, place and promotion.* Also called the "marketing mix," these variables are under the firm's control and can be configured and coordinated to achieve desired objectives most efficiently and effectively.

Product is a shorthand term for the firm's offering and is what *creates value* for consumers. It can be a true product, such as Skittles; a service, such as Princeton Review's GMAT Preparation Course; a place, such as Disney World; a person, such as Barack Obama; or an idea, such as the Southwest Climate Change Initiative.

After BP's Deepwater Horizon oil rig exploded off the Louisiana coast in April 2010 and spewed millions of gallons a day of oil into the Gulf of Mexico, restaurants, hotels and marinas in Pensacola Beach, FL, experienced high cancellation rates among people who mistakenly believed that the normally pristine white sand – a valuable component of the *product* – was awash in oil and tar balls. County commissioners allocated $700,000 in BP funds for advertising designed to counter the steep drop-off in tourism by showing beaches that were as clean and clear as consumers had always expected them to be.

Price represents the sacrifice customers must make in order to buy, use, or consume the product/service and is what *captures value* for the firm. Consumers around the world who purchased an iPhone 5 the day it was introduced gave up not only the money required to buy it, but also the time and energy associated with waiting in lines inside and outside stores.

Together, product and price determine how much value is created for consumers.

** Value = Benefits/Price **

The Patek Philippe Sky Moon watch, priced at $570,000, had a five-year waiting list of buyers just before it was introduced. Apparently the would-be owners believed that the watch's benefits, which presumably are status- and prestige-related, more than compensated for its unusually high cost.

The iPhone and Patek Philippe examples demonstrate the importance of marketers' setting prices that accurately reflect consumers' perceived value. Prices based on manufacturing costs, competitor levels, or profit targets might leave money in the pockets of consumers who believe the product/service is worth more than the firm is asking for it and who are even willing to wait for a chance to buy it!

Higher margins aren't about being greedy. Higher margins mean more money to invest in customers in the form of new product/service development, improvements to current products/services, enhanced customer experiences at retail and online, upgraded customer service, research, etc. Higher margins also mean more money to invest in better compensation and improved working conditions for employees, streamlined supply chain relationships, advanced production processes and equipment, and support for communities and causes.

Place gets the product to consumers when and where they want it and thereby *delivers value.* Place is a shorthand term for the company's distribution channel, which is part of the overall supply chain. The supply chain integrates all the activities, processes, people and firms involved in value delivery, starting with a manufacturer's order of raw materials from a supplier (e.g., Barry Callebaut is the world's largest cocoa processing company) and ending with the customer's purchase of the finished product. Within the supply chain are the channel members who handle a company's *finished* goods, such as wholesalers/distributors (e.g., Sysco Corp. is the world's largest food distributor) and retailers (e.g., Walmart, Carrefour and Tesco are the world's largest grocery retailers).

The Commercial and Consumer Equipment division of John Deere uses logistics management services provided by SmartOps Corp., which reported that its software helped the global agricultural machinery manufacturer reduce inventory by almost $1 billion and boost on-time shipments to dealers from 63% to 92% in the mid-2000s.

Promotion is the element of the marketing mix that *communicates value* to consumers. It also is a shorthand term, in this case one that encompasses all of a firm's marketing communications activities. Print, broadcast and online advertising; event sponsorship; point-of-sale displays; social media; direct mail; personal selling; consumer and trade promotions; publicity; public relations; buzz/word-of-mouth; cause-related efforts . . . these all are ways for a firm to reach, inform, educate and connect with its customers.

Despite the threat of an NFL lockout, eight months before the 2012 Super Bowl NBC had already sold 50 percent of the available advertising time slots, which cost more than $3 million for 30 seconds. Marketers recognize the unique opportunity the premier sports event offers to deliver messages to a highly engaged audience and be part of the hype and excitement associated with the broadcast.

Unilever's announcement that it would run an ad introducing its Dove Men+Care line of products during the 2010 game caused industry analysts to question the wisdom of such an expensive strategy. However, the gamble paid off. Prior to the Super Bowl, three of the most popular terms associated with Dove were "soap," "beauty" and "deodorant." A digital marketing agency reported that, 24 hours afterward, the brand's name was being paired in social media with "Super Bowl," "ad" and "men." Five months later, sales of the product line had exceeded company forecasts.

When each of the four Ps of marketing strategy is at its ideal point, and when the entire mix is integrated and synchronized, the result is a marketing plan optimized to achieve a firm's objectives. Such a plan will maximize the business' *top line* (sales revenue), *unit margin* (the difference between what it costs the company to make one unit of what it sells and the price at which the company sells it), and *bottom line* (profit).

Obviously, marketing can be a powerful player in a company's success. But marketing isn't omnipotent. It can't fix problems that aren't marketing-related.

For example, BP's plummeting stock price after the oil spill resulted in the loss of more than $110 billion in shareholder value. As long as the oil continued to gush from the well, no amount of marketing could repair the damage caused by the leak to the brand's reputation, image and financial condition.

Likewise, marketing can't eliminate the Israeli-Palestinian conflict, convince consumers to buy lawnmowers in January rather than May, prompt a switch from mobile phones back to the wall crank type, or boost sales of SUVs if fuel prices rise to $7 a gallon.

Marketing can – and should – design the right offering for the right customer, sell it at the right price at the right place, and communicate the right message about it in the right media.

In marketing, right makes might!

Chapter 2: Monitoring external conditions

Organizations don't operate in vacuums. The world of business is part of the constantly changing larger world. People are born and people die, leading to shifts in the demographic makeup of the global population. Innovative technologies are introduced that revolutionize industries and lives. Lawmakers pass legislation affecting business practice. Economic booms and busts lead to more or less spending, investment and job security. New competitors enter the marketplace. Issues rise and recede in the public consciousness. Consumer preferences evolve so that what previously was hot becomes obsolete, what once was completely unknown becomes cool, and what used to be popular becomes passé. The impossible suddenly becomes possible.

External events that are outside a company's control can have a significant impact on its ability to maintain customer relationships and engage in business as usual. Sometimes the events are sudden and unforeseeable, such as the 2010 BP oil spill that devastated individuals, companies, cities and states along the Gulf of Mexico coast. A few weeks after the explosion that caused millions of gallons a day to leak out of the well, a group of restaurants and several hotels in New Orleans filed separate class action lawsuits against BP claiming lost profits due to the city's tarnished attractiveness as a tourist destination. The decline in patronage they experienced wasn't the result of bad products, bad service, or bad marketing. It was the result of bad luck.

Other times the events aren't really events at all, but gradual occurrences that can be foreseen and anticipated. Nielsen estimates that the U.S. Hispanic segment will grow 167 percent between 2010 and 2050, compared to 42 percent for the total population. This growth rate is behind the Census Bureau's projection that in 2060, almost one in three Americans, or 31 percent, will be Hispanic. The buying power of Hispanics is expected to reach $1.5 trillion in 2015, prompting Walmart to convert two of its stores in Phoenix and Houston into Supermercados and open a Latino-themed warehouse store, Más Club, in Houston. Kroger fills the aisles of grocery stores in Hispanic neighborhoods with ethnic foods and staffs them with bilingual clerks. CNBC reported that although overall ad spending was flat in the first quarter of 2013, Spanish language TV and Hispanic magazines saw a 13.5 percent and 12 percent increase in ad revenue, respectively, as more brands spent more money targeting this attractive market sector.

For the New Orleans hospitality firms, the consequences of changes in market conditions were negative and unavoidable – a *threat* to their ability to create relationships with new customers and maintain and improve existing relationships. For Walmart, Kroger, and other brands, the effect was positive and planned for – an *opportunity* to create relationships with new customers and improve existing relationships.

Although there is no advance notice for accidents and acts of God, many forces and situations can be identified through continuous monitoring of the macro environment. The goal of monitoring is to gain information needed to plan for what lies ahead by making proactive adjustments to marketing strategy and/or tactics. Action, not reaction, is the key to creating, maintaining and improving mutually beneficial customer relationships.

What exactly does "monitor" mean, and what aspects of the external environment should be monitored? Marketers' early warning system isn't a sophisticated electronic device that can be aimed at the outside world to pick up signals of shifting market conditions. The most useful and important radar available to them is common *senses*: eyes and ears. Keeping both – or, rather, all four! – open is the best way to detect meaningful changes.

- Reading: current events, analyses of emerging trends, newsletters, reports, industry overviews, blogs, whatever publications target consumers are reading

    o These Web sites offer free information about consumer and market trends:

        ▪ https://iconoculture.com/US/Index.aspx

        ▪ http://springwise.com/

        ▪ http://trendwatching.com/

        ▪ http://www.pewinternet.org/

        ▪ http://www.google.com/trends

- Watching: TV, movies, videos, talk shows, social media, news programs, whatever target consumers are watching; what competitors are doing; observing target consumers as they buy, use and/or consume the product/service

- Listening: talking to target consumers, industry analysts, distribution channel members, suppliers, innovators/early adopters

What kind of information should marketers gather and compile when they're reading, watching and listening? Any and every kind that will help the company meet challenges, solve problems and exploit opportunities related to current or potential customers.

That's a lot of reading, watching and listening! Yes, but in reality, most circumstances with the potential to affect customer relationships fall into a few categories.

Socio-cultural factors

Population groups that comprise a culture have shared beliefs about the importance of certain concepts, conditions, or concerns. *Societal values* include freedom in the U.S., harmony in Japan, and love of nature in Nigeria (http://www.worldvaluessurvey.org/).

Sometimes broad shifts in attitudes toward a specific issue occur and unite people of different cultures who might otherwise be very unalike. For example, global warming/climate change and green marketing are interrelated movements that are part of the larger issue of environmental sustainability. Across the United States and around the world, companies and consumers are attempting to conserve natural resources, reduce waste, recycle packaging, cut down on carbon emissions, and take other steps to protect the well-being of the Earth's living and non-living systems.

The significance of the sustainability movement is evidenced by the fact that in 2009, *Newsweek* published its first ranking of green firms, based on environmental performance, policies and reputation. In 2012, IBM, Hewlett Packard, Sprint Nextel and Dell led the list of U.S. companies, while Santander Brasil (Brazil), Wipro (India), Bradesco (Brazil) and IBM were identified as the top-ranking global organizations http://www.thedailybeast.com/newsweek/2012/10/22/newsweek-green-rankings-2012-global-500-list.html. Interbrand, whose first ranking of the greenest global brands was issued in 2011, put Toyota (Japan), Johnson & Johnson (U.S.), Honda (Japan) and Volkswagen (Germany) at the top of its 2012 list http://www.interbrand.com/en/best-global-brands/Best-Global-Green-Brands/2012-Report/BestGlobalGreenBrandsTable-2012.aspx.

Consumer concern about the number of plastic beverage bottles that end up in landfills has helped fuel the rapid growth of SodaStream, which manufactures make-your-own-soda machines powered by compressed air. According to *Forbes*, sales of the countertop devices increased from $4 million in 2007 to $40 million in 2011. Today, the brand can be found on the shelves of such retailers as Walmart, Crate & Barrel, and Bed Bath and Beyond. (*Pssst. Should Coke and Pepsi be worried?*)

Not all issues have the enduring importance of the environment, but matters of less consequence can nevertheless have serious implications for marketers. The growth rates in the U.S. of single-parent households, alternative lifestyles and job "hopping," for example, aren't life or death issues, but could mean the end of a handsome salary for a brand manager who fails to spot the trends in time to implement strategic responses.

The *demographic* makeup of a population is another socio-cultural variable with marketing implications. Demographics are pieces of objective information used to describe and classify people, such as gender, race, ethnicity, education level, income and age. The fastest growing age group worldwide is seniors.

According to the U.S. Department of Health and Human Services, 605 million people around the globe were 60 years or older in 2000. The number is expected to be close to 2 billion by 2050, at which time seniors will outnumber children 14 and under for the first time in history. Think about the kinds of products and services seniors want and need, and how their consumer behavior differs from your own. When was the last time you considered having a facelift? How many blood pressure pills do you take every day? Have you ever toured a retirement community? Do you take ballroom dance lessons, play bridge, travel with tour groups or watch *Jeopardy!*?

The world is not only aging, but it's also growing. According to the Census Bureau's U.S. and World Population Clock (http://www.census.gov/popclock/), the current total global population is 7 billion, with 1.3 billion people living in China, 1.2 billion in India, and 316 million in the United States, where 80 percent of the population growth during the next 20 years expected to occur in Hispanic, African-American and Asian communities. The overall growth and the increase in diversity represent lucrative opportunities for marketers to forge new customer relationships at home and abroad.

Generational cohort is a term for a group of people born in the same time period who are in the same stage of life and have shared experiences that shape their values, attitudes, lifestyles and behaviors. Your parents are probably Baby Boomers, while you are most likely a member of Gen X or Gen Y (sometimes called Millenials). Baby Boomers tend to be materialistic, idealistic, and have a task-based view of technology. Xers are known for being independent, cynical, and comfortable with technology. Gen Yers tend to be civic-minded, realistic, and skilled at technological multitasking.

The different ages and experiences of the cohorts result in different levels of trust in institutions, marketing skepticism, savings-to-debt ratios, social consciousness and status orientation, among other dimensions. How does your consumer behavior differ from that of people you know who belong to other cohort groups? What implications do these differences have for marketing strategy?

Family structure is changing as couples wait longer to marry and have children, and as the number of single-parent, multigenerational, and nontraditional households grows. House design, school construction, day care services, and in-home nursing care are just a few of the industries affected by this shift.

Economic factors

What do economic growth rates, inflation rates, interest rates, and currency exchange rates have to do with marketing? They sound like the concerns of a company's finance department! While it's true that finance bears responsibility for hedging against the economic risk posed by fluctuations in those key measures, marketers must also be prepared for the effects of changes in a market's vitality on consumer behavior.

The key driver of economic growth is consumer spending. The collapse of several of the world's largest insurance and financial institutions in 2007-2008 and the resulting economic malaise plunged many countries, including the U.S., into a recession. Overall, consumers bought less because they had less money to spend and less confidence in the future. Even Walmart, famous for low prices, experienced a revenue and net income decline.

Although it might seem as if there's little a marketer can do in the face of a major assault on the economy, American Eagle is an example of a retailer that thought outside the box. Rather than automatically slashing prices to maintain market share, the company investigated ways to cut costs and pass along the savings to consumers. Eliminating the ribbon in the waistband of pants lowered manufacturing expenses, allowing the firm to reduce retail prices and protect store traffic – all while preserving all-important margins.

Small shifts often have far-reaching implications. Changes in interest rates affect home building and buying, which affect furniture retailers, moving companies, Realtors, decorators, home improvement stores, and appliance manufacturers. Those are the clear victims or benefactors, depending upon the direction of the change. But what about S.C. Johnson's Windex brand? More houses, more windows, more window cleaner. Or GE, which makes light bulbs? More houses, more lamps, more ceiling fixtures . . . .

On the other hand, fewer houses mean less wood, brick, concrete, siding, glass, hardware, plumbing pipe, electrical wiring and roofing material. But what about citronella candles? Lawnmowers? Sprinkler systems? Garden hoses?

With respect to currency exchange rates, companies with large overseas market shares can be hurt if the dollar strengthens against a foreign currency or helped if it weakens. And higher inflation results in lower real income and higher prices, which drive down consumer spending, which dampens growth, which leads right back where we started.

Technological factors

Few people would dispute the innumerable direct benefits provided by computers, cell phones, smart phones, e-readers, MP-3 players and a host of other technological gizmos and gadgets that improve consumer productivity, connectivity, and enjoyment of daily life.

Near field communication (NFC) technology enables electronic devices to communicate with one another using short-range radio frequencies, allowing a consumer whose smart phone contains an NFC chip to make purchases by simply touching the phone to a point-of-sale reader. However, in June 2013, research firm Gartner reduced by 40 percent its forecast of the 2012 – 2017 value of NFC transactions, citing slow adoption of the technology in all markets.

Technology also has indirectly affected consumer value delivery in a variety of other sectors. QR (quick response) barcodes in print ads or on billboards, buses, buildings, Web pages or business cards can be read (i.e., decoded) by cell phone applications to provide a variety of types of useful content (e.g., additional product/service/company information, payment options, retail locations, URLs) http://www.youtube.com/watch?v=B3lrcOhmp9g.

Radio frequency identification devices (RFIDs) attached to merchandise have enhanced coordination between suppliers and retailers, improving inventory control and decreasing the potential for stock-outs. And continuing advances in manufacturing automation, logistics planning and supply chain management drive down the costs associated with these business processes, allowing firms to pass the savings on to consumers in the form of lower prices.

One of the "dangers" posed by technology is its ability to reduce barriers to entry. Industries such as computer hardware, photography, and music recording and production all have seen increases in the number of small entrants who needed limited capital to begin operating.

A more widespread potential downside is the pervasive use of technology as a substitute for human beings, particularly in customer service delivery. The high frustration level of consumers forced to navigate seemingly endless sequences of push-button menus, only to end up listening to recorded messages, was the impetus for interactive voice response systems, or IVR, which allows callers to describe their needs orally. Automation is seductive because it can significantly reduce payroll costs, but companies that use it indiscriminately run the risk of destroying, rather than enhancing, customer value.

In addition to its general effects on business and marketing, technology can also have a profound impact on specific industries and companies. For example, the increased popularity of iTunes coincided not only with a drop in CD sales, but also with the demise of such retail chains as Tower Records and Wherehouse Music.

On the other hand, technology can help revive a low-growth category. Health monitoring devices, formerly known as bathroom scales, can now measure weight, fat content, hydration levels, bone mass, and even the amount of fat under the skin versus around organs. A basic scale can cost as little as $14, while a high-tech model that provides 19 different measurements can weigh in at a hefty $1,900 or more.

And then there are the Girl Scouts . . . . .

Consumers carry far less cash than they once did – a fact that didn't stop 200 troops in Ohio from boosting cookie sales during their 2011 drive. The girls used GoPayment (http://gopayment.com/), a free credit card reader by Intuit that clips onto smartphones, to sell such favorites as Thin Mints, Samoas/Carmel deLites and Tagalongs/Peanut Butter Patties at stands, booths and tabletops around the state.

Political/regulatory factors

Federal, state, local and even international governments frequently enact legislation and impose regulations that affect business practices.

Hospira Inc., the only U.S. maker of thiopental, an anesthetic used in lethal injections, had planned to shift production to Italy because of manufacturing problems at its North Carolina facility. However, Italy, which is one of the 27 nations in the 28-member European Union that have unconditionally abolished the death penalty (Belarus is the exception), wanted assurances the drug would not be used for capital punishment. Because Hospira couldn't provide such assurances, it halted production in 2011, leaving 34 death-penalty states scrambling for supplies.

Some laws are designed to protect consumers, such as the Consumer Product Safety Act, the Fair Packaging and Labeling Act, the Telephone Consumer Protection Act and the Clean Air Act. A quick search on the Internet will provide more information about what each of these entails.

Other laws safeguard companies from one another by preventing unfair competition, such as the Sherman Antitrust Act, the Clayton Act, and the Robinson-Patman Act, or by protecting patents, trademarks and copyrights.

Still others are designed to shield society from unbridled business activities, such as Sarbanes-Oxley and the Credit Card Accountability Responsibility and Disclosure Act.*

Consider how the various factors described above could impact the product/service, price, distribution, and/or marketing communications strategies of companies or industries with which you're familiar. For example, what significant current or coming changes in the market would you expect to be encountered by job search sites such as Beyond (http://www.beyond.com/), CareerBuilder (http://www.careerbuilder.com/), Execu|Search (http://www.execu-search.com/), GlassDoor (http://www.glassdoor.com/index.htm), Hound (http://www.hound.com/), TweetMyJobs (http://www.tweetmyjobs.com/), Simply Hired (http://www.simplyhired.com/), Jobserve (http://www.jobserve.us/), Idealist (http://www.idealist.org/), Indeed (http://www.indeed.com/), Internships.com (http://www.internships.com/), or Monster (http://www.monster.com/)? What could/should they do to plan for the changes in order to keep up with consumers and stay ahead of the competition?

In business, the only thing that's certain is change. Sometimes the impact of change can be easily predicted. But it's the not-so-obvious effects, those that trickle down or ripple over, that can catch complacent marketers by surprise. Marketers must be able to see the forest, the trees, and the horizon. Foreseen is forewarned, and forewarned is forearmed.

---

* It's likely that many of the acts would never have seen the light of day had companies and industries done a better job of regulating themselves. Ethical practices in all matters affecting consumers, competitors and society are the best protection against harm to any of those groups or to the company itself. Sooner or later, all unethical behavior has negative economic consequences. Unethical behavior also invites government restrictions that curtail the operational freedom of every firm in the barrel, not just the bad apples.

Chapter 3: Marketing ethics

More than 20 would-be, current or former academics are affiliated with Unemployed Professors.com, an Internet–based organization that offers writing and editing services to students "so you can play while we make your papers go away" (http://unemployedprofessors.com/).

The site, which even offers to produce dissertations required for doctoral degrees, instructs interested parties to "(r)egister at unemployedprofessors.com. Type your project into our user-friendly bidding form while eating ramen/drinking a beer/doing naughty things. Then watch, in amazement, as our Unemployed Professors voraciously outbid each other on your project so that they can buy themselves ugly clothing, or books."

Prices are also subject to bidding wars at We Take Your Class.com (http://www.wetakeyourclass.com/), where staffers promise that when they complete your online course, they'll "(d)o it all; tests, homework, discussions, projects and more!" Why? Because, according to a grammatically challenged banner on the homepage, "Life is too short to spend on classes you have no interest in."

The ethicality of students' submitting assignments that are the work of other people isn't up for debate. Doing so is cheating, plain and simple. But are the above-mentioned Web sites themselves unethical? If you believe they are, do you think Unemployed Professors is more unethical than We Take Your Class because it's staffed by academics who theoretically should know better?

Unlike laws, which are rules and regulations that can be enforced in court, ethics are moral principles and values that guide and govern the conduct of individuals and organizations. Potter Stewart, the late justice of the U.S. Supreme Court, characterized the distinction as, "Knowing the difference between what you have a right to do and what is the right thing to do."

The owners of sites offering academic help have a right to proffer such services, but whether it's the right thing to do is left up to individuals, not judges or juries, to determine.

Ethics are important not only in our personal lives, but also in all aspects of business. And they are paramount to marketing because the discipline focuses on forging long-term connections to customers, not on generating short-term transactions. Relationships depend on trust, which unethical practices destroy.

It is also marketing's province to communicate and uphold a firm's social responsibility, which refers to an organization's obligation to maximize its positive and minimize its negative impact on society. Proponents of corporate social responsibility (CSR) believe that firms should demonstrate proactive concern about the environment, community development, human rights, social issues and employee welfare. They contend that companies which value the idea of *doing good while doing well* gain a competitive advantage over those who don't, because they appeal to the growing numbers of socially and environmentally aware employees, investors and customers. Some corporate leaders, however, argue that metrics showing the link between CSR spending and market performance are necessary before CSR can become part of a company's business strategy.

The Boston College Center for Corporate Citizenship, in conjunction with the Reputation Institute, annually ranks the top 50 CSR companies in the U.S., based on a survey of almost 8,000 consumers. In 2011, the top 10 were Publix Super Markets Inc., Google, UPS, Kellogg's, Amazon, Berkshire Hathaway, FedEx, Campbell Soup Company, Baxter International, and 3M (http://www.bcccc.net/index.cfm?pageId=2202).

In acknowledgement of marketers' role as "stewards of society," the American Marketing Association created a Statement of Ethics delineating the professional values and norms that practitioners are expected to embrace. The Statement is included at the end of this chapter.

Marketing builds the brands that connect consumers to businesses and, therefore, is often the face of a company. You might not know very much about Mondelēz International, Inc. – the fact that it is a U.S. conglomerate employing 100,000 people around the world; that it is composed of the global snacking and food brands of the former Kraft Foods; or that the Mondelēz name came from Kraft employees, with "monde" being French for "world" and "delez" a substitute for "delicious." It's likely, however, that you are familiar with the company's brands: Oreo, Chips Ahoy!,Cadbury, Trident, Chiclets, Stride and others.

The brands that marketing builds generate most of the cash flows firms use to invest in customers and create wealth for owners. Because it's ultimately responsible for delivering consumer dollars, marketing often comes under attack for its competitive practices, which some people and groups believe create false needs and wants, foster materialism, produce cultural pollution, glorify sex and violence in advertising, make misleading or deceptive claims, reinforce stereotypes, exploit susceptible individuals or populations, promote consumption of unhealthy products and, in general, contribute to social ills.

That's a pretty long list of criticisms and complaints about a field whose purpose is defined as value creation! Part of the problem stems from the very reason that marketing is so important and powerful – people are different. They want different things, have different preferences and priorities, and see things differently. Hence, even in situations in which almost everyone is happy with what marketing is doing, there's always someone who isn't.

That doesn't mean marketing can figuratively throw up its hands and say, "Oh well, you can't please some of the people any of the time." For one thing, unhappy people can adversely affect a firm's ability to create wealth for owners. Two Stanford University researchers studied supermarket scanner data to determine the impact of a 2003 American boycott of French wine after France vocally opposed the war in Iraq. They found a 26 percent drop in U.S. sales at the boycott's peak, and an average 13 percent drop over the six-month event. A 2011 boycott of Target by lesbian, gay, bisexual and transgender consumers upset about the company's contributions supporting a gubernatorial candidate opposed to same-sex marriage caused a market capitalization decline of $1.3 billion – despite the fact that a prominent LGBT advocacy group gave Target a rating of 100 percent for workplace openness. And, according to the *Financial Times* (http://www.ft.com/intl/cms/s/0/e134401a-27ed-11e2-afd2-00144feabdc0.html#axzz2ZPvPQobn), a 2012 boycott of Japanese autos by Chinese consumers protesting Japan's occupation of islands in the East China Sea caused Nissan's, Toyota's and Honda's sales in that country to drop 35 percent, 49 percent and 41 percent, respectively.

For another thing, unhappy people can interfere with a company's efforts to create value for consumers. Protests by People for the Ethical Treatment of Animals led Ralph Lauren, Calvin Klein, Gap and Cole Haan to drop all fur products from their clothing lines and, according to an online Web site devoted to fur fashion, "coerced furs off the streets of New York" (http://www.furs.com/faq.html).

On the positive side, "discontents" can be the source of valuable insights regarding changing social mores and moods or potential improvements to products/services and marketing strategy. Six weeks after the release of *Super Size Me* by a documentary film maker who gained 25 pounds during a month of eating only McDonald's food, the company took large-portion items off its menu and introduced Go Active adult happy meals. Shortly thereafter, the corporation experienced its biggest sales increase in 17 years.

Industries that don't set their own limits on practices seen as questionable or unethical by vocal consumer groups leave themselves open to government intervention, which can result in stringent constraints. Santa Clara County, California, banned all toy handouts with meals that have more than 485 calories, 600 mg of salt and high fat or sugar content. The Center for Science in the Public Interest, a consumer advocacy group, has threatened to sue McDonald's if toys aren't removed from Happy Meals. The promotions are criticized for luring children into restaurants serving food that makes them obese as well as happy.

Whether you think of the toys as lures or as rewards, they're intended to enhance McDonald's value proposition and thereby draw more customers to the chain. By its nature, marketing is a persuasive process. The most effective marketing focuses on a target market composed of people who either do, or could, have an inherent appreciation for what the firm is offering. But even if they already value the product/service, they sometimes need a little nudge before they'll buy it, buy more of it, or buy it more often.

In the process of nudging consumers, potential ethical problems can arise with each component of a company's marketing strategy, some of which are clearly improper and others of which might be perceived as improper by individuals or groups. As you read the examples below, think about your own opinion regarding the "rightness" or "wrongness" of each, and about the potential impact on a firm's cash flows of the issue in question.

With respect to *products/services*, several issues can be of concern:
- Safety
  - In July 2013 alone, the Consumer Product Safety Commission announced recalls of dehumidifiers, electric smokers, LED lanterns, baby bath seats and other products http://www.cpsc.gov/. In each case, the recall was voluntary on the part of the manufacturer after a problem had been discovered. In 2008, however, the federal government indicted two Chinese nationals living in the U.S. and an executive of an American firm for knowingly importing and selling pet food containing melamine, an industrial chemical that led to the deaths of as many as 3,600 animals.

- Targeting: who is, and who is not, the aim of marketing strategy
  - Excluding consumer segments such as gays, racial minorities and the obese can be seen as unfair
    - According to NPD market research, plus-size clothing makes up only 17

percent of the ladies apparel market, despite the fact that 60 percent of women are overweight or obese.
  o Marketing Hooked on Phonics to children is non-controversial; marketing Honey Smacks cereal with 50 percent sugar to them is not.
  o Some people object to all targeting of children and teens, who control or influence billions of dollars in spending
    • Jezebel.com, a women's media Web site, tallied the prices of merchandise featured in the editorial content of one issue of *Teen Vogue* at $74,458.

• Other
  o Product proliferation, such as Crest toothpaste's 40 varieties, can confuse consumers and fill shelves with slow-selling items.
  o Planned obsolescence of older generation products, such as the Apple iPod, about which the late company founder Steve Jobs remarked that consumers who always want the latest and greatest should buy a new one at least once a year.
  o Misleading label information, such as Cocoa Krispies' box indicating that the cereal "helps support your child's immunity" yet contains 39 percent sugar by weight.
  o Wasteful packaging, such as individual bananas that some stores shrink wrap on Styrofoam trays.

Price issues include:
• Fixing
  o In July 2013, U.K.-based Barclays announced it would not pay a $470 million fine imposed by the U.S. Federal Energy Regulatory Commission for allegedly manipulating prices in the American electricity market.

• Discrimination
  o Airlines charge higher fares to business travelers who often buy tickets just prior to departure than to leisure travelers who generally purchase farther in advance.

• Gouging
  o After Hurricane Katrina, the attorneys general in affected states received complaints from consumers about higher-than-normal prices on car rentals, gasoline, plywood, motel rates, and bottled water.

Place issues can arise related to:
• Gray marketing
  o Kmart bought Swiss-made Accutron watches in Europe rather than from the company's authorized U.S. distributor because they were cheaper overseas.

• Slotting allowances
  o A Federal Trade Commission study found that introducing a new grocery product required $1.5 million to $2 million in up-front cash payments by a manufacturer to

each grocery store chain in order to gain shelf space. Retailers say the fees are required to cover the cost of making room in the warehouse for the product, programming the Universal Product Code (UPC) into the computer, and adding the product to the retailer's inventory system. But some firms contend that slotting allowances are unethical because they create a barrier to entry for smaller businesses that lack the cash flows necessary to compete with large companies.

- Bait and switch
  - o A Los Angeles carpet cleaner pled guilty to 10 criminal counts for advertising a $49.95 special to entice customers, then sending representatives who used bullying, intimidation and false statements to coerce them into paying hundreds more.

- Abuse of power and control
  - o Walmart's market share allows the retailer to demand rock-bottom prices from suppliers.

Potential problems associated with *promotion* include:
- Deceptive information
  - o The Federal Trade Commission imposed a $185 million judgment against "Your Baby Can Read!" for falsely claiming that its program could teach three-year-olds to read Harry Potter books, among others.

- Reinforcement of stereotypes
  - o A Sons of Italy report criticized media portrayal of Italian men as "uneducated, dishonest and/or violent," and women as "elderly, overweight housewives and grandmothers wearing black dresses, housecoats or aprons" (www.osia.org/documents/Advertising-Report.pdf).

- Unrealistic ideals
  - o Twenty years ago, the average fashion model weighed eight percent less than the average woman; today's models weigh 23 percent less.

- Stealth and guerrilla tactics
  - o When Sony Ericsson launched the first cell phone with an attachable camera, it hired actors to demonstrate the new product by pretending to be tourists in seven U.S. cities.

- Sex and violence
  - o Italian fashion house Dolce & Gabbana branded Spain as "behind the times" for demanding it withdraw a controversial ad showing a man holding a woman to the ground by her wrists while a group of men looks on.

- Spyware/adware and invasion of privacy

- A video by the American Civil Liberties Union communicates an apocalyptic perspective on the creeping erosion of personal privacy in the name of security http://www.aclu.org/technology-and-liberty/ordering-pizza-2015.
  - Web security firm McAfee Inc. estimates that three-quarters of the sites retrieved by user searches on such popular phrases as "free screen savers" or "digital music" attempt to install advertising software in visitors' computers.
  - Stopbadware is a non-profit organization supported by Google, PayPal, Mozilla and other companies that share the goal of eliminating spyware, viruses and other "bad software" http://stopbadware.org/.

- Spam
  - In 2003, Congress enacted the CAN-SPAM Act to curb unsolicited email and unwanted messages sent to wireless devices http://www.ftc.gov/spam/.
  - Spamhaus publishes the Register of Known Spam Operations, a database of evidence on 100 known spam senders and gangs worldwide http://www.spamhaus.org/rokso/.

- Junk mail
  - Catalog retailers, credit card companies and magazine publishers are among the types of firms that rely heavily on direct mail to communicate with current and prospective customers. In response to concerns about the volume of unwanted mail delivered, the Direct Marketing Association developed an online tool to help consumers control the amount and type of offers they receive https://www.dmachoice.org

- "Unmentionables"
  - K-Y Jelly has a TV ad campaign touting the product's ability to heighten sexual pleasure http://www.youtube.com/watch?v=KnmXG_hN6Hc.

Ethical issues can also arise with respect to a firm's broader impact on communities, society, and the planet. BSR (http://www.bsr.org/), which works with more than 250 member companies to develop sustainable business strategies, has identified several key social responsibility concerns. Notice that some are not solely in marketing's purview.

- Integrity of manufacturing, product quality
  - How and where items are made, their safety and suitability, and the environmental impact of manufacturing, use, consumption and disposal.

- Disclosure, labeling and packaging
  - Content, manufacturing process, packaging size and testing.

- Marketing and advertising
  - Scrutiny from consumers, regulators, nongovernmental organizations and media regarding targets, claims, cultural sensitivity and stereotypes.

- Selling practices
  o Uneven playing field for buyers versus sellers.

- Pricing
  o Lack of affordability for disadvantaged segments (e.g., elderly, poor, uninsured).

- Distribution and access
  o Lack of availability for disadvantaged nations, consumers.

Because what's ethical and OK to one person or group might not be perceived as ethical and OK by another, it can sometimes be difficult to know what direction to take in a business situation.

One critical rule should guide all decision-making:

Marketers should not engage in any behavior with the potential to:
- **Harm consumers**
- **Harm relationships with consumers**
- **Harm host communities**
- **Harm the company's future cash flows**

Between the media and consumer watchdog groups, it's a virtual certainty that firms engaging in unethical practices will be caught. The negative publicity that results typically has a deleterious effect on sales and stock price. Therefore, examining the actual or potential economic impact of a policy or decision can provide insight into the correct course of action for a company to take.

For example, in the late 1990s consumers angry over Nike's use of "sweatshop" labor in Third World nations protested outside stores and on campuses of universities with ties to the firm. Anti-Nike rallies were held in dozens of US cities and 12 different countries. Then-CEO Phil Knight's response to the protests was to defend the company, saying that working conditions in Asian factories had improved dramatically since Nike had begun doing business with them. Despite his frequent public reassurances, Nike's share price and sales revenue declined.

Faced with a 27 percent decrease in stock price, the company hired a vice president of corporate and social responsibility, upgraded its code of conduct and joined coalitions aimed at helping Third World workers. It now conducts regular random audits of factories and halts production in those that don't receive passing grades. After the policy changes, Nike's stock rebounded and, in 2010, hit an all-time high of $81.29. It currently trades in the $60s.

Imagine you were on the Nike marketing team charged with crafting a response to the protests. Being a loyal and faithful employee, and believing that your firm's practices weren't unethical, isn't it possible that you would have said, "We aren't doing anything wrong. We can't be responsible for working conditions in factories that manufacture products for a variety of companies. And it's only a vocal minority that's upset. Besides, those workers are making more money than they could get anywhere else in their country."?

That seems like a reasonable reaction. However, the truth is that it isn't about your opinion, or your principles, or even about the facts. Perception is reality. Your responsibility is to Nike's owners – the shareholders. And you must act in their interest, just as Nike ultimately did.

Luckily, the owners' interest is usually served by actions that also represent the greater good. Promoting a drug as a treatment for conditions not approved by the Food and Drug Administration might boost sales in the short run, but consumers harmed by the "off-label" usage can file class-action lawsuits that damage a pharmaceutical company's reputation, revenue and market value in the longer term.

Safeguarding a firm's financial interests requires safeguarding the interests of every stakeholder group. In the words of Wayne Calloway, the late CEO of PepsiCo, "It all boils down to this: results and integrity."

American Marketing Association
Statement of Ethics
Ethical Norms and Values for Marketers

PREAMBLE

The American Marketing Association commits itself to promoting the highest standard of professional ethical norms and values for its members (practitioners, academics and students). Norms are established standards of conduct that are expected and maintained by society and/or professional organizations. Values represent the collective conception of what communities find desirable, important and morally proper. Values also serve as the criteria for evaluating our own personal actions and the actions of others. As marketers, we recognize that we not only serve our organizations but also act as stewards of society in creating, facilitating and executing the transactions that are part of the greater economy. In this role, marketers are expected to embrace the highest professional ethical norms and the ethical values implied by our responsibility toward multiple stakeholders (e.g., customers, employees, investors, peers, channel members, regulators and the host community).

ETHICAL NORMS

As Marketers, we must:

- o Do no harm. This means consciously avoiding harmful actions or omissions by embodying high ethical standards and adhering to all applicable laws and regulations in the choices we make.

- o Foster trust in the marketing system. This means striving for good faith and fair dealing so as to contribute toward the efficacy of the exchange process as well as avoiding deception in product design, pricing, communication, and delivery of distribution.

- o Embrace ethical values. This means building relationships and enhancing consumer confidence in the integrity of marketing by affirming these core values: honesty, responsibility, fairness, respect, transparency and citizenship.

ETHICAL VALUES

Honesty: to be forthright in dealings with customers and stakeholders. To this end, we will:

- Strive to be truthful in all situations and at all times.
- Offer products of value that do what we claim in our communications.
- Stand behind our products if they fail to deliver their claimed benefits.
- Honor our explicit and implicit commitments and promises.

Responsibility: to accept the consequences of our marketing decisions and strategies. To this end, we will:

- Strive to serve the needs of customers.
- Avoid using coercion with all stakeholders.
- Acknowledge the social obligations to stakeholders that come with increased marketing and economic power.
- Recognize our special commitments to vulnerable market segments such as children, seniors, the economically impoverished, market illiterates and others who may be substantially disadvantaged.
- Consider environmental stewardship in our decision-making.

Fairness: balance justly the needs of the buyer with the interests of the seller. To this end, we will:
- Represent products in a clear way in selling, advertising and other forms of communication; this includes the avoidance of false, misleading and deceptive promotion.
- Reject manipulations and sales tactics that harm customer trust.
- Refuse to engage in price fixing, predatory pricing, price gouging or "bait-and-switch" tactics.
- Avoid knowing participation in conflicts of interest.
- Seek to protect the private information of customers, employees and partners.

Respect: to acknowledge the basic human dignity of all stakeholders. To this end, we will:
- Value individual differences and avoid stereotyping customers or depicting demographic groups (e.g., gender, race, sexual orientation) in a negative or dehumanizing way.
- Listen to the needs of customers and make all reasonable efforts to monitor and improve their satisfaction on an ongoing basis.
- Make every effort to understand and respectfully treat buyers, suppliers, intermediaries and distributors from all cultures.
- Acknowledge the contributions of others, such as consultants, employees and coworkers, to marketing endeavors.
- Treat everyone, including our competitors, as we would wish to be treated.

Transparency: to create a spirit of openness in marketing operations. To this end, we will:
Strive to communicate clearly with all constituencies.
- Accept constructive criticism from customers and other stakeholders.
- Explain and take appropriate action regarding significant product or service risks, component substitutions or other foreseeable eventualities that could affect customers or their perception of the purchase decision.
- Disclose list prices and terms of financing as well as available price deals and adjustments.

<u>Citizenship</u>: to fulfill the economic, legal, philanthropic and societal responsibilities that serve stakeholders. To this end, we will:

- Strive to protect the ecological environment in the execution of marketing campaigns.
- Give back to the community through volunteerism and charitable donations.
- Contribute to the overall betterment of marketing and its reputation.
- Urge supply chain members to ensure that trade is fair for all participants, including producers in developing countries.

<u>IMPLEMENTATION</u>

We expect AMA members to be courageous and proactive in leading and/or aiding their organizations in the fulfillment of the explicit and implicit promises made to those stakeholders. We recognize that every industry sector and marketing sub-discipline (e.g., marketing research, e-commerce, Internet selling, direct marketing, and advertising) has its own specific ethical issues that require policies and commentary. An array of such codes can be accessed through links on the AMA Web site. Consistent with the principle of subsidiarity (solving issues at the level where the expertise resides), we encourage all such groups to develop and/or refine their industry and discipline-specific codes of ethics to supplement these guiding ethical norms and values.

Chapter 4: Consumer behavior

Every organization, whether it be for profit, not for profit, or charitable, needs consumers. Or customers. Or clients. Or buyers. Or patrons. Or visitors. Or patients. Or donors. Or sponsors. Call them what you will, they are people who benefit in some way from their association with the organization. For example, one individual might contribute to the Boston Symphony Orchestra because s/he derives satisfaction from supporting cultural arts, while another might get similar satisfaction from contributing to the American Heart Association. Neither person is buying anything, but both receive value, in the form of positive feelings, through their affiliations.

Creating and delivering benefits to target markets is a critically important function of marketing. People don't buy toothpaste just to keep a tube of ingredients in their medicine cabinet. They buy it to get the benefit of whiter teeth, or fewer cavities, or fresher breath, or all three, depending on the brand. Those benefits are the answer to the consumer's unspoken question: *What's in it for me?* If I give you my money, what will I get in return? The *value* created by the product/service is the "WIFM."

The *right* customer

An organization can't offer products and services that everyone everywhere values, because people are different and seek different benefits from the things they buy, use, or consume. Nor can an organization offer products and services to everyone who values them, because some people aren't willing or able to pay an appropriate price for the benefits they desire. Consequently, an equally critical responsibility of marketing is finding the *right* customer for the organization.

Who is the right customer? The right customer is someone who not only gets value *from* an organization, but who also brings value *to* the organization by buying its goods/services at margin-preserving prices. No company can stay in business long if it gives consumers everything they want or need and gets little or nothing in return. Venture capitalists might be essential to getting an organization off the ground, but customer dollars are required to keep it going.

Consumers who will not purchase without a discount, who require significant or ongoing persuasion, or who demand costly levels of service lack an inherent appreciation for the product/service and, consequently, aren't worth pursuing or keeping. The problem isn't merely that the wrong customers fail to build value for the firm. Even more importantly, they consume resources that could be better spent on, or invested in, the right customers.

That's why marketing can be thought of very simply as the process of creating, maintaining and improving *mutually valuable* relationships with customers. Companies must identify the right customers from among all those in the product/service category and figure out the best way to deliver value to them through marketing strategy.

Too many organizations focus too much attention and money on beating their competitors, rather than on delighting their customers. For many years Coke and Pepsi were so worried about stealing market share from one another, they failed to notice that bottled water and alternative beverages were stealing share from them both.

Companies can't ignore competitors, but they should keep them in their peripheral vision and focus on their target customers. Staying abreast with, or ahead of, customers is the best way for a firm to stay ahead of the competition. This necessitates placing higher value on relationships than on transactions – on *share of wallet* than on market share. The former refers to the percentage of total spending in a category that a company/brand captures from existing customers. For example, if you spend an average of $20 a week on beverages and $10 of that total is for SoBe Lifewater, then that brand's share of your wallet is 50%.

The financial worth of a customer relationship can be determined through *customer lifetime value (CLV)* or *lifetime customer value (LCV)* analysis. The terms are used interchangeably to describe the net present value of the cash flows attributable to a customer over the length of his/her purchase history with a firm, less total acquisition and retention costs. The concept focuses on the importance of increasing the customer *retention rate* and decreasing the *defection rate*, because the cost of acquiring a new customer (e.g., offering a 0% annual percentage rate on credit cards for first-time applicants) is five to 10 times higher than the cost of retaining an existing customer (e.g., offering reward points).

At the most fundamental level, the objective of marketing strategy is to persuade target consumers to move from where they are – not purchasing in the product/service category at all or purchasing a competitor's brand, for example – over some hurdle to where the marketer wants them to be – purchasing the company's brand, for example.

The right mix of the four Ps can remove the hurdle by making the WIFM clear. But before a company can develop a marketing strategy that will influence its target consumers to move over, around or past some impediment to action, it first has to know what the impediment is and why it's in the way. Is it a lack of awareness that the brand exists? Inadequate knowledge or understanding about the brand's benefits? Unfamiliarity with the product or service category in general? Uncertainty about where to buy the brand? Beliefs that the brand is for other types of consumers? Failure to perceive a need for the brand? Exposure to negative word-of-mouth about the brand? Off-putting perceptions about the brand's image? Etc.

Answering these questions necessitates learning as much as possible about target consumers: what they think, know, perceive and feel; how they behave; who and what affects their thoughts, feelings and behaviors; when and where they buy/use/consume; and the "why" behind all of it. Once this is known, strategies can be developed to overcome their inertia, reluctance, or resistance.

** Understanding = influence **

Learning about the who, what, when, where, how and why – the psychology of marketing – is called the study of consumer behavior and helps companies:

- o Imagine, design and develop products/services that meet consumer needs and wants

- Despite the crowded competitive marketplace for casual clothing and athletic apparel, Kevin Plank, founder of Under Armour, http://www.underarmour.com/shop/us/en/, achieved $725 million in sales of moisture-wicking sportswear in 2008, just 11 years after the company was founded.

o Make those products and services stand out from the competition in consumers' hearts and minds
  - *Fast Company* says the Under Armour brand name is synonymous with performance apparel.

o Choose brand names and package designs that facilitate consumer decision-making
  - "Under Armour" communicates the idea of competitive battle.

o Determine how many varieties of a product or service to offer
  - Under Armour's success in apparel led to the launch of shoes for specific sports and, in 2009, running shoes aimed at attacking Nike's dominant share of the $5 billion U.S. market.

o Set a price that communicates and captures value
  - NPD reports an average price for sports shoes of $48; Under Armour shoes sell for $85 - $120.

o Distribute products and services through the most effective channels
  - Under Armour launched sunglasses in 2006 and, three years later, signed a distribution deal with online retailer FramesDirect.com that allows the brand to reach more customers.

o Communicate with consumers about products and services
  - The core elements of Under Armour's marketing communications strategy are advertising, media relations/PR, in-store merchandising and relationship-building with professional and amateur athletes and teams at all levels. In fact, the brand's Web site allows consumers to submit sponsorship requests directly to the company.

The examples above illustrate how an understanding of consumers ends up being reflected in a company's marketing strategy. But where does an understanding of consumer behavior start?

It starts with YOU, me, and all the people in the marketplace who are consumers. Every consumer brings a set of attitudes, beliefs, thoughts, feelings, perceptions and behaviors to the purchase and/or use of products and services. Let's break down the elements of, and influences on, your search for, selection, purchase, use, evaluation and disposition of the things you buy.

- *Are you buying to fill a need or to satisfy a want?* This is sometimes referred to as the *problem recognition* stage of the consumer decision-making process. You might need lead refills for a mechanical pencil you'll use on a finance exam, but you probably don't need a Snickers bar after lunch. You simply want it! Likewise, you might not need new running shoes for the Marine Corps Marathon because your current ones are adequate, but you might want a pair of Asics Gel Kayano 15s after learning that a friend cut three minutes off his total time by wearing them. Needs, wants – you simply require or desire additional value from the marketplace.

- *Will you gather outside information to use in decision-making?* Once you've recognized your value gap, you'll seek ways to fill it. In the *information search* stage of the process, you'll either rely on past experience and memory (referred to as an *internal search*), or you'll conduct an *external search*. For example, if you're buying a candy bar, you'll probably select a favorite brand out of habit or try a new brand on impulse, without checking external sources for facts about its ingredients or nutritional content. On the other hand, if you're deciding which cruise to take after graduation, you'll likely check with travel agents, Web sites, brochures or friends. In most product/service categories, the Internet has significantly reduced the time and effort associated with external search.

- *What criteria will you use to evaluate your options?* Let's say you're thinking of cruising to the Bahamas, Cozumel, or Aruba. These three options are known as your *consideration set* because they comprise the only destinations in which you're interested. For whatever reason(s), you're not considering going to Alaska, the Mediterranean, or Scandinavia. You put together a quick spreadsheet to compare your options and decide to base your choice on sail dates, on-board activities, special package deals, and weather forecast on the island. The dimensions you use to make your final selection are known as *evaluative criteria* and represent your means of assessing value.

- *How will you decide?* It's unlikely that you'll close your eyes and pick a cruise out of a hat, any more than you chose a school by throwing darts at a map. The *purchase decision* stage of the process can be simple or complex, depending on characteristics of the decision-maker and of the product/service category. If you stop by the vending machine to buy a candy bar to eat while evaluating your cruise options, your choice is likely to be *routine* (I always buy Snickers) or *impulsive* (I'll try the new M&M's Minis). If the vending machine also contains five different kinds of Lipton Cup O Soup and you suddenly realize you're pretty hungry, you might engage in *limited problem-solving* in which you first decide between a candy bar and soup, then decide which flavor of soup you want. But your choice of a cruise engenders a higher level of involvement and, therefore, is likely to involve *extended problem-solving.* Unlike a candy bar or soup, a cruise is an intangible experience that can't be picked up and examined; it is "bought" infrequently so you can't rely on history alone in making your choice; it has a higher purchase price, which increases the risk associated with a bad decision; and more people will likely be involved in the overall purchase.

- *Who else is involved in the decision and in what role(s)?* You might be the *initiator* who came up with the idea of a cruise, but the friends or family with whom you're traveling might be *influencers* on the destinations you're considering. Once you narrowed the choice down to three options, you might give up your chair in front of the computer and leave the final choice to a *decision maker,* perhaps the person in the group who has been on the most cruises. Your parents might end up being the actual *buyer*, because they agreed to pay for the cruise as a graduation present. And you might book passage for someone who had nothing to do with any part of the decision but wants to be a *consumer* of the cruise because "it sounds like fun."

- *What personal factors influence your purchases?* Enough about the cruise; let's move on to other product categories! As a student you might think a two-seat sports car is the perfect automobile. But as a father with three children, you undoubtedly would want and need a bigger vehicle. Likewise, as a student responsible for paying your own tuition, you might be happy wearing casual clothing from Target. As a successful investment banker, however, you might prefer Chanel suits. In fact, a variety of demographic factors – age, income, gender, race, and education – affect consumers' buying behavior.

- *What psychological factors influence your purchase?* Applying Maslow's Hierarchy of Needs framework to marketing allows us to recognize that consumers have different *motivations* for buying different products and services. They can buy for simple, straightforward reasons having to do with taking care of themselves and their bodies. They can also buy for less obvious reasons related to how they feel about themselves and their place in the world. Drinking a bottle of Gatorade after a workout fills your *physiological* need for replenishment. Carrying Jogger Fogger pepper spray on a run fills your need for *safety*. Joining a club fills your *social* need to belong and be loved. Taking a preparation course for the CPA or CFA that improves test performance fills your need for *self-esteem*. Owning a Harley-Davidson fills your need for *self-actualization* by demonstrating that your full personal potential has been maximized.

  Consumers' *perceptions, attitudes, beliefs,* and *knowledge* levels also influence their purchases. For example, if you aren't in the market for a video game console, you might ignore all information you come across from Sony about PlayStation 3, Nintendo about the GameCube, and Microsoft about Xbox 360. You don't perceive differences among the brands because you don't pay attention to advertising about them. In fact, you might have a totally negative attitude toward video games because you know someone who got hooked on them and had to leave school after his grades plummeted. Or you might actually believe video games can help improve concentration and reflex time for some people. You might know a great deal about video game consoles and the features each brand offers, or you might know nothing about video game consoles, period. Your perceptions, attitudes, beliefs and knowledge all affect your *ability* to make purchases in a product or service category (i.e., video game consoles).

Thus, even if you're willing (i.e., motivated) to buy an item, you might not have the ability to do so because you lack the fundamental antecedents of purchase.

- *What external factors influence your purchase?* *Situational factors*, which refer to the physical environment in which purchase occurs, can have a significant impact on buying behavior. The lighting, noise level, clutter of products and promotional messages, and time and energy available to you affect your purchase *opportunity* and, hence, determine what, whether, where and how you buy.

  Social factors also affect your purchases. Every culture shares a set of values, beliefs and norms that shape consumption. For example, the drive for individualism that might manifest itself in clothing choices is stronger in the United States than it is in some Asian nations, where conformity is valued more highly. Cultures can be based on a number of dimensions, including religion, national boundaries, and global regions. Within every culture exist subcultures that further influence purchases. Coin collector, jazz-lover, MG owner . . . the list of subcultures that help define who you are can be endless. Your family, roles typically associated with your gender, social class, and the groups with which you affiliate or want to affiliate also affect your consumption behavior.

- *When and where will you purchase?* Once a decision has been made, a consumer still must determine when to make the purchase (will you make a special trip to buy a new set of ear buds for your iPod, or wait to pick them up when you're already out?) and where to buy (which retailer will get your business?). The choice of retailer can involve another search and evaluation process.

- *What is your post-purchase evaluation and behavior?* Sometimes consumers think more about a decision after purchasing than beforehand because they fear they made the wrong decision (I should have bought the Bianchi bicycle instead of the Fuji). The feeling of buyer's remorse is referred to in psychology and marketing as *cognitive dissonance*. Warranties, money-back guarantees, after-sales communications, 800-numbers and online customer service are some of the means by which marketers can reduce cognitive dissonance. They want you to tell others about the wonderful new product/service you purchased, not about what a terrible mistake you made!

The bottom line is: The more marketers know about consumers, the better they'll be able to create, maintain and improve mutually beneficial relationships with them.

- o Who are they in terms not only of demographics – age, gender, education level, race, and income – but also of psychographics – the values, interests and lifestyles that help describe and define them?

- o How do they make decisions – quickly or deliberately?

- o What are the stages in the decision-making process – recognizing the need or desire to buy, gathering information about alternatives, deciding what options will be considered in the choice and what the evaluation criteria will be, making the final choice, deciding where to buy the good or service, and so on?

- o What's the sequence of the stages and how long do they last?

- o Who (people) and what (psychological, situational, and social factors) are influences on the decision and when do the influences occur?

- o Once they've made and consumed/used/experienced the good or service, to whom do they talk about it and what do they say?

Knowing the answers to these questions helps ensure that the company will deliver the right benefits to the right customer and thereby maximize the value to both parties. Where does a marketer find the answers? The answer to *that* question is coming up!

First, however, a few words about another very important consumer type – businesses. Organizations that purchase goods and services for their own use or for resale comprise what's known as the business-to-business market. B2Bs include institutions such as schools and hospitals; manufacturers who buy raw materials to produce offerings for end consumers (e.g., you and me); wholesalers, distributors and retailers who sell the offerings produced by manufacturers; and the government.

Let's use Ford automobiles to illustrate the B2B market.

- o Every F-150, Taurus, Focus, Explorer, or Expedition that comes off the assembly line is manufactured from inputs such as fiberglass, steel, leather and plastic supplied by other businesses. *Ford is a customer of those suppliers.*
    - ▪ Ford buys inputs in the quantities required to manufacture just enough vehicles to satisfy the needs of its own customers. Thus, the suppliers are said to experience *derived demand* because their sales depend on demand for Ford vehicles in the market of ultimate consumers.

- o Before consumers can buy F-150 off showroom floors, Ford has to sell the truck to dealers. *The retail dealerships are Ford's customers.*

o Not only does Ford sell individual vehicles to individual consumers, but the company also sells fleets of vehicles to local, state and federal government agencies, as well as to corporations with sales forces. *Those agencies and corporations are also Ford customers.*

Ford operates in both the B2B and the B2C (business-to-consumer) market, and recognizes that the behavior of buyers between the two differs significantly. B2B markets are characterized by larger sales, greater product complexity, higher buyer expertise, closer buyer-seller relationships, longer selling cycles, and the involvement of more people in the purchase process.

Consider the example of carbon fiber reinforced polymer, which is a type of fiberglass used to make high-end racing vehicles. If Advanced Composites Group, a manufacturer of CFRP, wanted to convince Ford to begin using the product, the company would face a challenge far greater than that faced by a part-time employee at Dick's Sporting Goods trying to sell a pair of running shoes to a consumer.

The vice president of marketing at Advanced Composites would have to figure out the name of the appropriate individual to contact in the Ford organization, get through to the secretary or administrative assistant who acts as the person's gatekeeper, schedule an appointment to see the individual, and then make a personal visit. When the VP arrived at the Ford employee's office, s/he would undoubtedly find several other people in the room, all of whom will have a say in the decision.

Assuming the Ford folks had any interest whatsoever in making the switch, they'd have to turn the issue over to engineers for study. If the engineers gave it the go-ahead, production people would be brought in to talk about implications for the manufacturing process. Necessary changes to the assembly line would have to be made.

Once all relevant Ford people had given a thumbs-up, Ford would seek bids from other manufacturers of CFRP by putting out a request for proposals for what undoubtedly would be a multi-million-dollar purchase. When all the suppliers had submitted bids, a buying committee would study the proposals and make a selection. Then a committee would prepare order specifications detailing the exact product requirements, prices, delivery dates, penalties for non-performance, etc.

The buying process literally could take years to complete and, in the end, Advanced Composites might not even win Ford's business. Meanwhile, the part-time employee at Dick's Sporting Goods finished school and opened a Hampton Hotel franchise!

Despite differences between B2B and B2C buyers, the key to success is the same in both markets: understanding the *who, what, where, when, why* and *how* of their behavior.

As Sam Walton, the late founder of Walmart, noted, "Only the consumer can fire us all." Keeping your job means always keeping his remark at the top of your mind and always keeping the consumer at the heart of your business mission!

Chapter 5: Marketing research

Before they can create value for consumers, marketers need to know what consumers value. They learn this through marketing research. Some people think of marketing research as the process of collecting *information* about consumers. But information is like a chunk of magma that contains a diamond. The real value of research – the precious gem – comes from the *insight*s that can be mined from the raw data.

Insights are the proverbial light bulbs in the brain that click on when you figure out something you hadn't been able to figure out before. In the marketing realm, such "aha" moments occur when marketers understand their consumers in ways they hadn't previously understood them. This requires approaching research not as an information-collection exercise, but as an intelligence-gathering mission, the objective of which is to discover hidden "secrets." However, secret insights aren't the ultimate goal; strategic direction is. Unless they are used in the development of superior marketing strategies, insights are no more valuable than the raw data from which they were extracted.

Consider these examples:

After purchasing Folgers Coffee Co. in 1963, Procter & Gamble researched consumers' coffee-drinking habits, preferences and perceptions. The information was the basis of ad campaigns positioning Folgers as the solution to life's problems the kindly Mrs. Olson recommended to her neighbors, and as a premium coffee that could be served at the nation's finest four-star restaurants. However, the brand remained a marginal player behind #1 Maxwell House.

In 1984, P&G marketers analyzing additional consumer research had an insight that helped Folgers overtake its rival and reach $1 billion in sales: *Coffee is about waking up.* The realization led to the development of an ad campaign that featured the line "The best part of wakin' up is Folgers in your cup" in a jingle and showed people smiling as they were awakened in the morning by the smell of freshly brewed coffee. The brand's market share grew from 17 percent to 36 percent, largely because of one simple "aha!" distilled from huge volumes of data http://www.thewisemarketer.com/features/read.asp?id=82.

Right now you might be thinking, "That's easy and obvious." But it isn't either. Just ask the California Milk Processor Board, whose members had been experiencing a steady, long-term slide in milk consumption in the 1980s and early '90s. For years the Board had sponsored the "Milk Does a Body Good" ad campaign, which increased the number of consumers who believed drinking milk was healthy to 90 percent. Yet sales continued to sag. And although positive beliefs and attitudes are important, it's sales that ultimately matter.

Research by a new ad agency found that people thought milk was boring and drank it as an accompaniment to sweet and sticky foods. That information sparked an insight: *Milk alone is blah, but having to eat certain foods without milk is upsetting.* The "deprivation" idea was the inspiration behind the "Got Milk?" campaign, which is credited with not only halting the decline in consumption, but also increasing sales. In the campaign's very first ad, a history buff whose apartment is crammed with items commemorating the Aaron Burr-

Alexander Hamilton duel receives a call from a radio station offering $10,000 if he knows who shot Hamilton. He answers correctly, but because his mouth is full of peanut butter and he has no milk to wash it down, his response is unintelligible. The ad was named one of the 10 best commercials of all time in a *USA Today* poll.

In both examples above, consumers supplied information, marketers extracted insights, the company/cooperative altered its positioning strategy, and cash flows increased. That's the value of marketing research!

Market research and *marketing* research are sometimes used as interchangeable terms, even though they really aren't. The former deals with the analysis of markets – their sizes, segments, growth rates, competitive structures, etc. The latter is a broader pursuit that can include market research, but also encompasses the study of consumers – their demographic and psychographic profiles, decision-making processes, beliefs, attitudes, behaviors, preferences, influences, etc. Marketing research results are used to pinpoint problems, identify opportunities, formulate marketing plans, calibrate the marketing mix, monitor performance and, in general, guide managerial decision-making.

The marketing research process can consume significant time, money and energy. It can also expose a firm to the risk of competitive preemption by delaying new product/service launches or alerting rivals to planned strategies. For these reasons, research shouldn't be undertaken simply to learn things you'd *like* to know. There's no such thing as perfect information in terms of either quality or quantity. Managers who try to track down every last detail before choosing a course of action suffer from "analysis paralysis," an affliction that will undoubtedly hurt their careers . . . and their companies' success!

What might an effective manager actually *need* to know? Below is a lengthy, but certainly not exhaustive, list.

- Market-related information
    - Size, growth rate, shifts and trends
    - Total forecasted demand
    - Competitor market shares, budgets, strategies and performance
    - Barriers to entry
    - Likelihood of new entrants
    - Opportunities and/or threats in business environment

- STP-related information (i.e., segmentation, targeting and positioning)
    - Segments, sizes, growth rates, trends
    - Target customer's demographic and psychographic profile
    - Benefits desired
    - Choice process
    - Satisfaction with value delivered by brand
    - Competitive brand positions

- Product-related information
  - Ratings of current brands in market on relevant dimensions
  - Packaging innovation, trends, evaluation
  - Potential new products/services
  - Potential new uses/users/usage occasions for existing products/services
  - Evaluation of new product/service ideas
  - Brand awareness and recall
  - Brand image/personality perceptions
  - Brand name selection

- Price-related information
  - Price elasticity of demand
  - Price-benefit tradeoffs
  - Analysis of costs, margins, profits
  - Reference prices
  - Acceptable prices

- Place-related information (i.e., related to distribution channels)
  - Sizes, market shares and growth rates
  - Innovation and trends
  - Service support and quality
  - Marketing support
  - Site selection

- Promotion-related information (i.e., related to integrated marketing communications)
  - Advertising copy testing
  - Advertising recognition, recall and liking
  - Sales promotion response rates
  - Sales force compensation
  - Awareness, trial and repeat purchase levels
  - Impact of celebrity endorser
  - Word-of-mouth content and rate

Think about your lemonade stand and the information you might want and/or need your customers or potential customers to provide. Knowing the most appropriate sugar content, preferred hours of operation, optimal location and perhaps even the desirability of a loyalty program could enhance your ability to create value for lemonade lovers and, thereby, for you.

However, before conducting research, you – and all marketers – should address a series of questions, each of which will be described subsequently:

1. Why is the information needed, i.e., what's the research objective?
2. What are the budget and timeframe?

3. What kind of data will be collected – secondary, primary; qualitative or quantitative?
4. How will the data be collected – focus group, interview, projective techniques, questionnaire/survey or experiment?
5. What sampling method will be used – probability (simple randomized, stratified or clustered) or non-probability (voluntary, quota or convenience)?
6. How will the data be analyzed?
7. Who will incorporate the findings in decision-making?

Regarding #1 above, remember that a marketer should conduct research only when necessary. For example, if you have all the business you can handle at your lemonade stand and the percentage of repeat customers suggests a high level of satisfaction with your operation, you don't need anything other than informal input from your buyers: "Wow, that sure is delicious and refreshing!" If, on the other hand, you notice a drop-off in sales, you have to find out the reason for the decline before you can reverse it. Consequently, identifying and defining the research question is the first step in the marketing research process.

In 2004 Dove, which is owned by Unilever, launched the Campaign for Real Beauty, an integrated marketing program celebrating physical variations in women. Prior to the launch, the brand had been looking for a way to position itself in a culture that "perpetuate(d) an idea of beauty that was neither authentic nor attainable." Dove commissioned The Real Truth about Beauty study to achieve its research objective of "further(ing) the global understanding of women, beauty and well-being – and the relationship between them."

Because marketing research can be resource-intensive, the budget and timeframe should be set in advance to avoid sticker shock. It can cost as much as $7,500 to recruit participants and hire a moderator for one focus group session. Surveys cost an average $40 per respondent by phone, up to $7,000 for 200 responses by mail, and up to $5,000 by email http://www.entrepreneur.com/marketing/marketresearch/article55680.html.

Once the objective, budget and timeframe have been determined, the marketer then should specify the type of data required. Two kinds of information can be gathered in marketing research: secondary and primary.

Secondary data already exist and were collected from *internal* and/or *external* sources. Internal sources include a company's profit and loss statements, balance sheets, sales figures, sales-call reports, invoices, inventory records and prior research reports. External sources include the government (e.g., U.S. Census Bureau http://www.census.gov/), periodicals, books, and commercial suppliers (e.g., SymponyIRI http://www.symphonyiri.com/, Forrester http://www.forrester.com/rb/research, and Nielsen http://www.nielsen.com/us/en.html), the Internet (e.g., Pew http://www.pewinternet.org/, MarketingCharts http://www.marketingcharts.com/, eMarketer http://www.emarketer.com/, HubSpot http://www.hubspot.com/marketing-resources/, and Google Insights http://www.google.com/insights/search/#).

Secondary data are relatively fast and inexpensive to compile – you don't even have to leave your desk!

Before designing the Real Truth study, Dove commissioned a literature review that examined existing research on beauty, appearance and self-worth from 118 countries in 22 different languages.

Primary data are original and collected directly by the marketer. There are two types, qualitative and quantitative, which differ in terms of the number of people who participate in the study (i.e., the size of the sample, or subset of the population of interest) and whether the participants are chosen through probability sampling or nonprobability sampling. With the former, each member of the population of interest has a known, non-zero chance of being included in the sample, while with the latter the chance of an individual being included in the sample is unknown.

Qualitative research is typically used for preliminary, exploratory purposes. It usually involves a small number of respondents and is designed to provide information depth, rather than breadth. Because of the limited sample, the findings have no statistical significance and can't be generalized to the whole population. Participants in qualitative research are selected via nonprobability sampling, often based on convenience (individuals are easy to find and recruit), a pre-set quota (at least 20 or 30 or . . . people), or their willingness to volunteer.

Examples of qualitative techniques include focus groups, which are interactive discussions among eight to 12 people led by a moderator; one-on-one interviews, which are 20-60-minute unstructured (or loosely structured) face-to-face or telephone conversations between a researcher and an individual; and projective techniques, such as word association, sentence completion, picture interpretation and role playing, all of which are designed to elicit participants' underlying motivations and attitudes.

One year after launch, focus groups suggested that the Real Beauty campaign was changing women's perception of the brand from old-fashioned to contemporary.

Quantitative research is used to draw statistically significant conclusions that can be generalized from the sample of participants to the greater population of interest. Consequently, such studies involve large numbers of participants selected through probability sampling that can be either simple randomized (all participants have an equal chance of being chosen from the population), stratified (individuals are placed in groups based on some characteristic, e.g., gender, and each person has an equal chance of being chosen from the group), or clustered (individuals are placed into groups, e.g., veterans in 15 metropolitan areas; one group is randomly chosen, e.g., veterans in Detroit, and all members of the chosen cluster are included).

Quantitative data are typically gathered using surveys or questionnaires administered by mail, telephone, email, Web or in person via "intercept" (catching passers-by at the mall, the grocery store, etc.). Experiments are another form of quantitative research in which a marketer investigates the impact of a change in one factor (the independent variable) on another (the dependent variable).

In the 2004 Real Truth about Beauty study, Dove conducted 3,200 telephone interviews with 18-64-year-old women in 10 different countries to assess their perceptions of their own beauty and of beauty as a concept. In the brand's 2006 Beauty Comes of Age study, 1,450 women aged 50-64 from nine different countries were surveyed to reveal stereotypes associated with beauty and aging. And in the 2008 Real Girls, Real Pressure study, 4,373 American girls aged 8-17 were surveyed to understand their self-acceptance, confidence and emotional orientation.

Illustrations of different types of questions used to gather information appear at the end of the chapter.

In the last several years, the rise in social media, Web-based activities, and mobile marketing has fueled a veritable data explosion. Powerful new tools facilitate the transformation, analysis and packaging of millions of millions of pieces of raw data (referred to as *terabytes*), resulting in unprecedented opportunities to study, understand and influence consumers, as well as support tactical and strategic decision making.

Prior to the advent of *big data*, as the gigantic databases are often called, marketers generally had ideas or hypotheses regarding the behavior of consumers and collected data to support or refute those notions. *Data analytics* turns the process on its ear, allowing researchers to mine datasets for patterns and connections that otherwise would go unimagined and undetected.

The science of data-driven decision making is the subject of Michael Lewis' book, *Moneyball: The Art of Winning an Unfair Game*, and the 2011 movie *Moneyball* starring Brad Pitt. Both detail the use by the Oakland Athletics – a team with a $41 million payroll competing against the likes of the New York Yankees, with a payroll of $125 million – of sabermetrics (derived from the acronym SABR, for the Society for American Baseball Research) to put together a winning team based on player statistics most strongly correlated with offensive success. The Athletics' analysis showed that on-base and slugging percentages predicted wins far better than traditionally used numbers such as runs batted in and batting average.

MC Hammer, the rapper, dancer and entrepreneur, says analytics is "the end game" of behavioral targeting, revealing where his fans are going, what they're doing and how best to invest his marketing money http://www.youtube.com/watch?v=k6aBITJuSQA.

Before collecting data, the marketer should know how they will be analyzed. A discussion of analytical techniques and programs is beyond the scope of this class. Suffice it to say that conjoint analysis, regression, factor analysis, multidimensional scaling, analysis of variance and cluster analysis are several of the techniques available.

Among other results, Dove's data analysis revealed that only two percent of women around the world describe themselves as beautiful; 97 percent of older women believe that society is less accepting of appearance considerations for women over 50 compared to their younger counterparts; and 62 percent of girls feel insecure or unsure of themselves.

What was the outcome of the Real Beauty program that Dove launched based on insights culled from the research data? The campaign returned $3 in sales for every $1 spent on marketing and won an unprecedented number of Cannes advertising awards http://psucomm473.blogspot.com/2009/03/dove-campaign-for-real-beauty.html. In the first six months, sales of the brand's firming products increased 600 percent in the United States and 700 percent in Europe. By the end of the first year, global sales surpassed $1 billion, exceeding company expectations http://www.brandrepublic.com/news/217970/oms-real-women-ads-dove-sees-sales-soar-700/. Moreover, the Dove page on Unilever's Web site reports that the campaign has been featured in more than 800 articles in leading newspapers and magazines and shown on more than 25 major TV channels http://unilever.com/brands/personalcarebrands/dove/index.aspx.

Clearly, Dove didn't simply ask consumers for their input and opinions. Marketers also listened to what consumers told them. Most importantly of all, they acted on the information. In doing so, they enhanced value for the target market and the firm's owners.

Research that isn't used to glean the insights necessary to provide strategic direction is a waste of time – for the consumer and the company. Data are nothing more than bits of raw material. But a good marketer can always find ways to make data talk!

ASK consumers.

LISTEN to consumers.

ACT on what consumers tell you.

Closed-ended questions

Dichotomous
Have you ever visited Italy?
◊ Yes ◊ No

Multiple choice
Which one of the following products have you purchased from Best Buy?
◊ CD ◊ Camera ◊ Cell phone ◊ Computer
◊ DVD ◊ Flat-screen TV ◊ Flat-screen TV ◊ Printer

Semantic differential scale
Zappos.com's Web site is:

Easy to use	: ___ : ___ : ___ : ___ : ___ :	Hard to use
Fun	: ___ : ___ : ___ : ___ : ___ :	Boring
Modern :	___ : ___ : ___ : ___ : ___ :	Old-fashioned
Friendly	: ___ : ___ : ___ : ___ : ___ :	Unfriendly
Laid back	: ___ : ___ : ___ : ___ : ___ :	Pushy
Soft sell	: ___ : ___ : ___ : ___ : ___ :	Hard sell
Helpful	: ___ : ___ : ___ : ___ : ___ :	Unhelpful

Note: Placing all the positive adjectives on the left-hand side may encourage a subject simply to check the extreme left or right of the scale. On the other hand, subjects might fail to notice if some items are reversed.

Likert scale
"Zappos.com is very easy to learn to use compared with other shopping sites."

Strongly Disagree	Somewhat Disagree	Neither Agree nor Disagree	Somewhat Agree	Strongly Agree

Intention-to-buy scale
How likely is it that in the holiday season you'll buy a gift for someone from Target.com?
◊ Definitely will buy
◊ Probably will buy   Note: This question is difficult to answer
◊ Might or might not buy   unless asked in November or December.
◊ Probably won't buy
◊ Definitely won't buy

Importance scale
How important is it for you that online retailers include shipping in their selling prices?
◊ Extremely important ◊ Very important ◊ Somewhat important
◊ Not very important ◊ Not important at all

<u>Rating scales</u>
Zappos.com's Web site is:

  ◊ Excellent

  ◊ Very good

  ◊ Good

  ◊ Fair

  ◊ Poor

On a scale of 1 to 10 where 10 is excellent and 1 is a dog, how would you rate the Zappos.com Web site? _____

Open-ended questions

<u>Completely unstructured</u>
Walmart has been sued for failing to promote women to top management positions. What is your opinion of Walmart's product assortment?

> Note: This starts with a negative comment that is unrelated to Walmart's product assortment. It will create more criticism and is thus biased.

The most important consideration for me in choosing a smartphone is:

> Note: The number of lines in a question can affect the length of the response.

<u>Word association</u>
What is the first word that comes to mind when you hear "Harley Davidson"?

<u>Sentence completion</u>
When I choose a new car, the most important factor in my decision is _____.

<u>Story completion</u>
I ate Ben & Jerry's ice cream the other day. As I was eating it, I swirled my spoon around in the bowl. Doing this made me think and feel . . . .

<u>Picture completion</u>
A picture of two characters is presented, with one making a statement in a "thought balloon." Respondents are asked to identify with the other character and fill in the empty thought balloon.

<u>Thematic Apperception Test</u>
A picture is presented to respondents, who are asked to make up a story about what they think is happening or might happen in the picture.

Chapter 6: Segmentation, targeting and positioning

Segmentation, targeting and positioning, or STP, are the critical foundation of marketing strategy. Once a firm makes STP decisions, developing strategies for the four Ps – product/service, price, place and promotion – is an easier process. Knowing the consumer you want to target and the brand promise you want to make to him or her helps you rule out ideas that would be inconsistent with the target, or with the brand promise, or with both.

To illustrate the fundamental importance of STP, let's suppose a new neighbor moves into the apartment next door to you. He has just obtained his cosmetology license and wants to open a hair salon targeting undergraduate college students. When he finds out you're enrolled in a marketing course, he asks for feedback on his plans. He says he intends to carry a full line of expensive perms and dyes, serve wine to clients, charge $60 for basic cuts, open his salon in a mall 15 miles from the university, and advertise in the city newspaper.

What do you tell him? Presumably that he needs to rethink his marketing strategy because his product/service, price, place (location) and promotion plans don't fit the needs, wants, behaviors or abilities of undergraduates!

If the company doesn't know who the right customer is or what the right promise is to make to that customer, marketing is inefficient and ineffective, and the budget might just as well be bet on a Martian winning the Mixed Martial Arts Ultimate Challenge. Successful marketing plans begin with careful consideration of STP decisions – the way a large market is divided into smaller segments, the choice of one or more segments to "woo," and the distillation of the brand's benefits down to a unique and valuable consumer promise.

Segmentation: cutting up

Look around your marketing class and think about some of the things you have in common with the other individuals in the room: At the very least, you're all students, about the same age, attending the same university, and taking the same course. You're an attractive market for many marketers who are interested not only in your purchasing power, but also in the benefits of having educated, savvy, upwardly mobile consumers buying, using, consuming and/or wearing their brands.

Now think about the ways the class can be divided into smaller groups of similar individuals: Gender, height, home state, birth order, favorite spectator sport, number of energy drinks consumed each day, model of car driven, mother's first name, TV channel watched for news, religion, type of computer owned, brand of candy eaten most often, rank in high school graduating class, age when attended first live concert . . . and the list goes on.

Some of the dimensions would be meaningful to marketers, while others would not. For example, Red Bull definitely would want to know who the heavy consumers of energy drinks are, and M&M's could benefit from finding out what the most popular candy among students is. On the other hand, knowing that five students in the class had mothers named Sarah wouldn't be at all useful to a marketer.

The world is a huge place, populated by more than 7 billion people. No manufacturer can sell to every individual because it would be impossible to reach them all and because there isn't a product or service on the planet that every single individual would want to buy or consume. Moreover, as mentioned in the chapter on consumer behavior, even if all the inhabitants of the planet did want to buy or consume a particular brand, the marketer wouldn't want to sell to all of them. For one thing, not everyone would or could pay the asking price. For another, selling to a mass market might not be consistent with the brand's image. If you asked 100 people if they would like to own a Rolex, 99 of them might say, "Yes!" But it's unlikely that all 99 could afford the watch. In addition, if 99 out of 100 people did own a Rolex, the brand's image of exclusivity and status would suffer. As a result, fewer people would be interested in buying one.

Segmentation is the process of dividing a market of consumers into separate, smaller groups that are similar on some underlying dimension(s). Think of it as slicing and dicing, just as you would a potato – you can cut it into big chunks or tiny cubes. Markets, too, can be split any number of ways into homogeneous clusters that are easier and less costly to reach and influence than one gigantic mass.

Demographic criteria such as age, gender, income, education, marital status, family size and life cycle, occupation, nationality, ethnicity and religion are commonly used to segment markets, particularly as a first cut. For example, when you were born, banks and insurance companies probably contacted your parents to sell them products and services typically desired by individuals starting or expanding their families. Savings plans, insurance policies, and college funds are of special interest to young parents. At the other end of the family life cycle, builders of zero-lot-line houses (those with small, low-maintenance yards) are interested in identifying adults who want to down-size after their children leave home.

The benefit of demographic information is that it's easy to obtain. To find tabular data for countries and regions, as well as demographic indicators, population pyramids and source information for nations around the world, log on to the U.S. Census Bureau at http://www.census.gov/population/international/data/idb/informationGateway.php. Nielsen offers a variety of segmentation services, including PRIZM, P$YCLE, and ConneXions, all of which can be accessed at http://www.claritas.com/MyBestSegments/Default.jsp.

The drawback of demographic segmentation, however, is that it's a broad-based approach that doesn't take into account the many ways in which humans of the same age, gender, income, education, etc., differ from one another.

Imagine you've graduated and you and your best friend were hired by the marketing departments for two different manufacturers of denim jeans. Coincidentally, each of you has been given the task of developing a print advertisement to help the company introduce a new brand of jeans into the competitive U.S. market.

Suppose your boss described the target market for your company's jeans as: Males, 18-24-years-old, who have at least a high school diploma and earn a minimum of $22,000 a year. Now suppose your best friend's boss described the target market for their company's jeans in a different way: Males who drive pick-up trucks, are politically conservative, hunt and fish at least twice a year, own a shotgun and subscribe to *Field & Stream*.

Which of you will have an easier time developing an ad that "speaks" to the target market? Undoubtedly, your best friend. The demographic description your boss gave you applies to lots of young men, whether they're preppies or rednecks, rich or poor, liberal or conservative, bookworms or outdoorsmen. The description given to your best friend, on the other hand, allows her to get a vivid picture in her head of the person she's trying to reach.

Because demographic similarities don't help marketers figure out what makes a group of people "tick," they often turn to psychographic descriptors such as those provided by your best friend's boss. *Psychographics* are based on the assumption that the products and services a person purchases and the media s/he consumes reflect the individual's personality characteristics, values, interests, attitudes, opinions, and lifestyles. These factors cut across demographic boundaries. For example, the Republican Party is a group of people of all ages, races, ethnicity, incomes and education levels who share similar beliefs about politics and the role of government in our lives. Likewise, (RED) is a movement supported by millions of demographically diverse individuals with a common goal of eliminating AIDS in Africa.

A drawback of psychographic information is that it's more difficult than demographic data to obtain. Numerous research firms compile psychographic data, but it can be expensive to purchase. If you visit http://www.strategicbusinessinsights.com/vals/presurvey.shtml, you can take the VALS survey, which places U.S. consumers into one of eight psychographic segments based on the primary motivation for their behavior (ideals, achievement, or self-expression) and their resources (physical and psychological).

A good example of the use of both demographic and psychographic segmentation variables is cable TV. Spike is aimed primarily at men, while women are Lifetime's and Lifetime Movie Network's main target. The History Channel, Golf Channel and Discovery Channel, on the other hand, cut across gender and are based on interests and activities.

In the B2B market, segmentation is based on characteristics of organizations rather than individuals. Common bases include:

- Geographic
    - Population density: urban, suburban, rural
    - Region: north, south, east, west, Midwest

- Demographic
    - Number of employees
    - Annual sales
    - NAICS (North American Industry Classification System) code: identifies companies according to type of economic activity/industry

- Purchase conditions and situation
    - Evaluation criteria
    - Order size
    - Type: new buy, modification of a previous buy, straight rebuy

- Relationship
    - Values
    - Risk profile
    - Loyalty

Businesses can also be described in terms of their purchase behavior. Common segments are:

- ◆ Programmed buyers who engage in routinized purchasing
- ◆ Relationship buyers who remain loyal as long as the price is reasonable
- ◆ Transaction buyers who are always ready to switch suppliers for a better price
- ◆ Bargain hunters who are both price- and service-sensitive

Regardless of whether it's a B2B or B2C market, slicing and dicing it into smaller segments allows a company to home in more precisely and cost-effectively on customer needs and wants. A segmentation scheme should produce clusters that are *identifiable* (you must know that consumers are out there who meet the segmentation criteria), *measurable* (you must be able to find those consumers and figure out how many there are), *sizable* (there must be enough consumers in the segment to make it worthwhile to market to them), *accessible* (it must be cost-effective to reach them via marketing communications) and *actionable* (consumers must be predisposed to respond favorably to your marketing efforts).

Here's an example, albeit a crazy one, to illustrate these concepts. Let's say you've come up with the bright idea of selling a DVD of a physics professor demonstrating how to use a slide rule. {What on Earth is a slide rule (http://sliderulemuseum.com/)?!?!} You want to market the DVD to blue-eyed college students who were high school valedictorians, are now majoring in quantum mechanics, and whose families own Portuguese water dogs.

Are there consumers out there who meet all of those segmentation criteria? Who in the world knows? Even if they do exist, how will you find them and figure out how many of them there are? Even if you could figure out the size of the segment, isn't it likely to be extremely small? Even if it were large, what media could you use to communicate with them cost-effectively? Even if you could reach them, aren't consumers in the segment unlikely to purchase a DVD about an obsolete device? The segment isn't *identifiable, measurable, sizable, accessible* or *actionable*!

Segments should be based on the opportunity to maximize return on investment and profitability. When finer segmentation produces clusters that cannot be reached efficiently and effectively, the marketer has gone too far. Just as a potato can be cut into pieces so tiny they are essentially drops of liquid containing just a grain or two of starch, so, too, can a market be sliced too thinly.

In his book *American Sniper*, the late SEAL Chris Kyle describes the U.S. Army's segmentation of terrorist groups in the city of Ramadi, Iraq: hard-core Islamist fanatics; locals who were less fanatical but nevertheless wanted to kill Americans; and opportunistic criminal gangs making a living off the chaos (p. 285).

Segmentation is essential to – but not exclusive to – marketing.

Targeting: zeroing in

While segmentation entails slicing and dicing a large market into smaller pieces, targeting involves evaluating the attractiveness of the various segments and zeroing in on one or more. "Attractiveness" isn't determined simply by looking at characteristics of the target market. It requires identification of a match between what the brand offers or can offer – its promise – and what a particular consumer segment wants or needs – the benefits they value.

Wealthy individuals with high disposable income might be attractive in general because of their buying power, but they are not an attractive segment for Solo disposable plastic cups because wealthy individuals do not want to buy or use large quantities of Solo cups. Undergraduate students, on the other hand, do. Thus, undergraduates with limited incomes would be a more desirable target market for Solo than wealthy individuals would be.

Although finding a match between the brand's benefits and consumer wants is a necessary condition for selecting a target market, it is not sufficient. Suppose there were 15 people in the world, or 150, or even 1,500, who loved slide rules so much they were willing to pay $100 for a device that had been priced at about $25 in its heyday. The maximum revenue potential from the segment would be $150,000, which isn't very much, period, but would be especially paltry once salaries, overhead, marketing and other costs were deducted.

What about the target market for, say, interactive video games? Angry Birds has been downloaded a record 1.7 billion times for 99 cents by "casual" *mobile device gamers*, while Call of Duty: Black Ops II, which retails for $40 - $60, smashed the record among "serious" *console gamers* with $1 billion in sales in 15 days. Although the casual segment is significantly larger, serious gamers are willing to pay significantly more for what they judge to be a higher-quality experience. In terms of innovation, however, it is easier to develop, release and upgrade mobile content quickly. Clearly, there are many factors to consider when selecting a target market, including the company's goals and competencies.

Attractive segments are sizable, offer growth potential, produce positive returns on investments, and provide the firm with opportunities for brand differentiation. Segments that meet these criteria are "attractive" because they allow companies to maximize return on investment and profitability.

Chris Kyle reports the Army's conclusion that hard-core Islamist fanatics "had to be eliminated because they would never give up" and, thus, would be the primary focus of the upcoming assault. At the same time, the Army would work with tribal leaders in an effort to persuade fanatical locals and opportunistic criminal gangs to leave or quit killing (p. 285).

Positioning: narrowing down

Once a company has zeroed in on one or more segments to target, it must decide which of the brand's benefits will appeal most to consumers in those segments. Positioning is a way of describing or defining a person, place, product, service or idea in a way that explains what it's all about to a relevant audience. If you asked a room full of random people how many were pro-abortion, it's likely that very few would raise their hands. However, if you asked the same people how many were pro-choice, more hands would probably be raised. The movement has been "positioned," or framed, as pro-choice, making it about a woman's right to decide, rather than as pro-abortion.

A brand's position tells consumers what it stands for or means and what value it promises to deliver. It's the result of narrowing down all the positive aspects of a brand and highlighting the specific benefits that are most valuable and compelling to the target market and that differentiate the brand from competitors. A position answers the all-important question, "If I buy Brand X, what's in it for me that's different from or better than what I can get from Brand Y?" Consequently, it's the basis for the WIFM or brand promise.

BMW automobiles are safe, luxurious and dependable. Any one of these characteristics could conceivably underpin the brand's position. The problem is that Mercedes, Infiniti, Rolls-Royce and Bentley also are safe, luxurious and dependable. On the other hand, "the ultimate driving experience" positions BMW uniquely in its segment as the car for people who truly enjoy driving, like feeling the road beneath them, and see an automobile as more than a means of getting from one place to another in comfort and style.

The Disney brand is all about three primary benefits: fun, family and entertainment. Everything that bears the Disney name should deliver that promised value bundle and thereby reinforce the brand's image and position. Although a chain of day-care centers or a children's hospital might have a great deal of appeal for parents who trust the Disney name, neither service would offer the three benefits at the core of the company's image.

Firms often use an internal brand concept/brand positioning statement to delineate the brand's benefits and the target consumers who value them. The statement requires marketers to zero in on the value proposition that will appeal to the target market and differentiate the brand from competitors. The basic format is:

(Brand name) is the (name of the product/service category or segment in which the brand competes) for (psychographic target market) that offers (primary consumer benefit(s)) because it has (delineation of specific product/service features that support/provide evidence of the benefit(s)).

For example, suppose a company were introducing a new brand of liquid spiced butter and, after extensive market research, decided to market it to people who eat popcorn (rather than, say, to gourmet cooks, or people who like to grill, or individuals who are heavy consumers of bread and muffins, or . . . .). The concept statement might be:

"Sputter! is the liquid spiced butter for popcorn lovers that offers a convenient way to add hot, mouthwatering flavor to every bag or bowl of popcorn because it comes in three zesty varieties (garlic parmesan, sour cream and onion, and cinnamon sugar) packaged in microwavable, easy-pour pouches."

- Brand name
    - Sputter!
- Product category/segment in which Sputter! will compete
    - Liquid spiced butter
- Target market
    - Popcorn lovers, a *psychographic* target that cuts across age, income, race, education, religion, geography . . . .
- Benefit(s)
    - Convenience; hot, mouthwatering flavor

- Product features that support/provide evidence for benefits
  - Convenience: microwavable, easy-pour pouches
  - Hot: microwavable
  - Mouthwatering flavor: three zesty varieties

The concept statement clearly identifies the target market of popcorn lovers and the value proposition of convenience and hot, mouthwatering flavor. Some brand marketers are reluctant to focus on a particular segment of consumers because they want to go after "everyone," and they're hesitant to emphasize just a few of the brand's benefits because they want to offer "everything." However, such brands usually get lost in a market of competitors with clear positions. Oldsmobile, Mercury and Pontiac failed in part because they couldn't convince enough consumers that they offered value the other car brands didn't.

A brand can position itself in the hearts and minds of target consumers:

1. By feature or benefit
   a. Skype offers free long-distance calling http://www.skype.com/intl/en-us/home
   b. Trident Layers gum is a flavor sandwich
      http://www.tridentgum.com/#/products/layers/strawberrycitrus

2. By use or application
   a. Febreze freshens fabrics http://www.febreze.com/en-us/pages/home.aspx
   b. Paypal is for online shopping https://www.paypal.com/

3. By user
   a. USAA provides insurance to military personnel and their families
      https://www.usaa.com/inet/ent_logon/Logon?redirectjsp=true
   b. Campagnolo products are for serious cyclists
      http://www.campagnolo.com/jsp/en/index/index.jsp

4. By product/service category
   a. Taco Bell encourages consumers to "think outside the bun"
      http://williamwayland.com/case-studies/taco-bell/
   b. Netflix is more convenient than bricks-and-mortar video rental stores
      http://www.netflix.com/

5. By competitor
   a. Aleve works longer on arthritis pain than Extra Strength Tylenol
      http://aleve.com/
   b. Dunkin' Donuts says hard-working people prefer its coffee to Starbucks'
      https://www.dunkindonuts.com/

6. By price or quality
   a. Tiffany claims to have the best diamonds http://www.tiffany.com/?siteid=1
   b. At Dollar Tree, everything's $1 or less http://www.dollartree.com/home.jsp

7. By cultural symbols
    a. McDonald's Golden Arches are strongly associated with the fast-food restaurant http://www.mcdonalds.com/us/en/home.html
    b. The Jolly Green Giant is an icon in the canned and frozen vegetable aisles http://www.greengiant.com/

The above examples of positioning strategies demonstrate possible approaches for encapsulating and communicating a brand's value to target customers. In most cases, however, brands don't fit neatly or exclusively into one category. For example, Rolls-Royce is a high-quality, high-priced brand (#6) that offers super-luxury (#1), is targeted at the ultra-wealthy (#3) as an alternative to all other "lower-rung" vehicles (#4) and a direct challenger to the Bentley (#5), and whose symbol has become synonymous with excellence (#7). If you had to pick just one approach, though, you'd probably pick super-luxury. Strong brands have strong meanings.

Marketers must be very careful choosing a positioning strategy because it determines how consumers will see the brand relative to competitors. Nuprin hired Jimmy Connors, a veteran tennis champion and Maria Sharapova's coach, as a spokesperson for the pain reliever because he represented the brand's target market: aging athletes who experienced muscle aches and pains after playing sports or exercising on the weekend. Nuprin became the #1 brand in the muscle aches and pains segment of the market. The problem was, the segment was very small relative to those for cold and flu, arthritis, and headaches. When consumers experienced muscle aches and pains, they reached for Nuprin. When they experienced other, more common problems, however, they reached for other brands.

Regardless of the particular strategy or combination of strategies employed by marketers, consumers ultimately see brands in terms of benefits, which can be perceived at different levels:

o Functional benefits (performance-based)
    ▪ Pledge polishes my furniture http://www.pledge.com/
    ▪ I can call friends around the U.S. on my Droid http://www.droiddoes.com/

o Experiential (sensory-based)
    ▪ I love the smell and look of a room after I've used Pledge
    ▪ I like the way the Droid feels in my hand

o Psychological benefits (emotion-based)
    ▪ I'm happy when Pledge makes my furniture shine
    ▪ I really enjoy talking with friends on my Droid

o Symbolic benefits (principle/value-based)
    ▪ Pledge helps me have an attractive home and that's important to me
    ▪ I value the friends I've had since elementary school and my Droid makes it possible for me to keep those friendships alive

Of course, a brand's benefits can be perceived or translated differently by different consumers. Some people buy Apple computers because they are simple to operate – a functional benefit – while others buy them because Apples allow them to be more creative – a psychological or symbolic benefit. Some people patronize Starbucks because they like the brand's fair trade stand – a symbolic benefit – while others enjoy sitting in the stores doing homework or chatting with friends – an experiential benefit.

As a student interested in starting or enhancing your career, it's important to think about *your* personal brand position. What are you all about? How are you different from other individuals who might be interviewing for the same internship, job or promotion? What value do you bring to the table?

According to Tom Peters, a management consultant and author of *The Little Big Things* and *The Pursuit of WOW!,* "It's time . . . to take a lesson from the big brands, a lesson that's true for anyone who's interested in what it takes to stand out and prosper in the new world of work" http://www.fastcompany.com/magazine/10/brandyou.html.

If someone gave you 30 seconds to write down the first three thoughts that come to mind when you hear the name of the movie *The Hangover*, you could probably do it without any trouble.

What if someone gave you 30 seconds to write down the three top benefits you would bring to an employer? Or the three adjectives that best describe your work ethic?

For what do you stand? For what can others count on you? If you can't supply the answers to these questions as quickly as you can identify the benefits of your favorite candy bar or automobile, then it's time for you to start thinking about the most important brand you'll ever build and use in your life: *YOU.*

STP applies to products, services, places, ideas, and people. STP applies to you! Slicing up, zeroing in and narrowing down – segmentation, targeting and positioning – are the keys to communicating the right value proposition to the right customer, which, in turn, is the key to strong relationships and business success.

Chapter 7: New product/service development

The very best companies – the ones most attractive to investors, employees, and other stakeholders – don't simply survive; they thrive. Achieving the goal of vitality, rather than mere viability, requires growth.

One of the financial measures used by Wall Street analysts when assessing a corporation's performance is *profit*, which is the difference between the total money coming in from customers, i.e., the firm's *sales revenue*, and the total money going out, i.e., the firm's *costs*.

Sales revenue is often referred to as the "top line" because it appears at the top of a company's income statement, while profit is often referred to as the "bottom line" because it appears – you guessed it! – at the bottom.

Given that Profit = Total Revenue – Total Costs, a company can achieve profit growth two ways: a.) by increasing sales revenue, which entails selling more units of the product or raising the price per unit, or b.) by cutting expenses. Although marketing has an impact on costs, one of its primary functions is to boost top-line sales revenue.

Let's assume a firm wants to increase revenue without raising prices. Its other alternative is to *sell more units*, which can be done through three basic approaches:

1. Selling more of its current offerings to existing customers
   - SUBWAY offers special prices for combining a sandwich with a drink and chips or cookies http://www.subway.com/subwayroot/index.aspx

2. Finding more customers
   - SUBWAY implemented a school lunch program that includes both on-site locations and off-site catering services

3. Developing more products/services for:
   - Existing customers
     - o SUBWAY introduced salads to give customers an alternative to sandwiches
   - New customers
     - o SUBWAY's personal-sized pizzas were designed to appeal to Pizza Hut and Domino's customers

An easy way to think of these growth strategies is *more purchases*, *more people*, and *more products*. However, if the company focuses on creating more sales, rather than on creating customer value, the increase will be a temporary spike from additional *transactions*, rather than a permanent increase due to new or improved *customer relationships*.

In order to sell more of its *current* products/services to existing customers – #1 above – a firm must motivate them to:

1. Consume/use more of the product/service when they consume/use it
   - As an alternative to the drink and chips or cookies mentioned above, consumers could buy a foot-long SUBWAY sandwich rather than a six-inch

2. Consume/use the product/service more often
   - Increase the number of times each week a SUBWAY meal is eaten

3. Consume/use the product/service in more ways
   - Cut SUBWAY sandwiches into bite-sized pieces and serve them as appetizers

These can be summed up as *more product, more often, more ways*. In each case, consumers should gain additional value through increased use/consumption. For example, SUBWAY could deliver more value to customers who purchase foot-longs by giving them free insulated sandwich bags (imprinted with the company's logo, of course!) in case they want to eat one half and save the other half for later. To increase value for consumers who enjoy SUBWAY but whose desire for variety prompts them to eat meals elsewhere, the company could offer new salads and sandwiches "for a limited time only" to stimulate interest and additional visits. And store signage, printed napkins and information on the company's Web site could educate consumers about ways to simplify entertaining by serving SUBWAY products.

Alternatively, a firm can boost sales to existing customers by improving its current offerings or by developing new (i.e., more) products/services, both of which are known as product development. For example, Gatorade has introduced a variety of flavors (lemon-lime, frost, lemonade, cool blue, citrus cooler, fruit punch, and orange) and formulations (for concentration, metabolism and protection), as well as protein and nutrition shakes.

Increased sales can also be the result of attracting new (i.e., more) customers by taking current products/services into new segments (e.g., targeting Gatorade to senior citizens) or by developing new products/services for entirely new markets (e.g., the Gatorade In-Car Drinking System designed to keep professional race car drivers hydrated throughout races). The former is known as market development, the latter, diversification.

		Product/service	
		New	Existing
Customers	New	Diversification	Market Development
	Existing	Product Development	Focus

All of these strategies offer growth potential for a company. However, the remainder of this chapter will focus on the one that's essential to maintaining and improving relationships with existing customers and creating relationships with new ones.

New product/service development, or NPD, is a key component of customer value creation because it helps ensure that a firm's offerings meet the evolving needs and wants of its target consumers. According to Peter Drucker, a management theorist and consultant who wrote numerous books on business, "when the change outside is greater than the change inside, the end is near." In a marketplace characterized by shifting consumer preferences, increasing competition, and an accelerating pace of technological advancement, companies that don't innovate are at risk not only of decreased sales and market share, but also of eventual extinction.

Innovation can occur in manufacturing processes, distribution channels, support services, business models, strategic networks and alliances, and a number of other areas related to a company's operations. But it is product/service innovation that allows a company to satisfy and delight customers and thereby stay ahead of the competition, expand retail presence, respond to changes in the business environment, and achieve growth.

Frito-Lay introduced toasted corn Doritos in 1966, followed by taco-flavored in 1968 and nacho-cheese-flavored in 1972. Today the brand line includes chile limon, nacho picoso, flamas, enchilada supreme, ranch dipped hot wings, spicy chipotle BBQ, cool ranch, nacho cheese, salsa verde, spicy nacho, spicy sweet chili, taco, and tapatio http://fritolay.com/our-snacks/doritos.html.

Why so many varieties? Well, imagine your own Doritos-eating habits. Suppose only one type was available – toasted corn. Even if you absolutely loved them, wouldn't you occasionally get tired of the same old same old and crave something different? Or suppose you began developing a taste for spicy flavors. Would you continue to buy as many bags of toasted corn as you once had? What if a competitor, say Pringles, introduced a line-up of new flavors that included barbecue, cheeseburger, chile con queso, chile y limon, French onion dip, honey mustard, jalapeno, loaded baked potato, Memphis BBQ, pizza, ranch, salt & vinegar, salsa de chile habanero, and sour cream and onion (http://www.pringles.com/products/flavors)? Mightn't you be tempted to forget your love of and loyalty to Doritos and buy a canister? Or what if increased demand for corn as a raw material in alternative fuels led to a steep increase in the price of toasted corn Doritos. Isn't it possible that you'd quit buying the snack altogether and switch to potato chips?

In all of the hypothetical situations above, Doritos' ability to deliver value to you would be adversely affected. In reality, an aggressive product development strategy has helped the brand avoid such potential problems and become the number one snack chip in the United States. It has stayed ahead of the competition by staying ahead of – or at least abreast of! – its customers' wants and needs.

Product/service development encompasses varying degrees of innovation, ranging from new-to-the-world on one end to repositioning on the other.

Art Davie and Rorion Gracie created a new-to-the-world customer experience when they staged the first Ultimate Fighting Championship event in 1993. The partners didn't invent mixed martial arts fighting, but their sports entertainment breakthrough launched an industry that in 2012 generated 10 of the top 15 pay-per-view events, surpassing both boxing with four and WWE with one.

An example at the other end of the spectrum is Cadillac, an automobile that was first sold in 1902 and over the years had come to be known as a luxury car for successful retirees and old men. The introduction of the Escalade SUV in 1998 helped reposition the brand as a car for hip, affluent Baby Boomers. For the first five months of 2013, Cadillac experienced its largest sales increase since 1976, making the 110-year-old car the fastest growing major automotive brand in the U.S.

In between the new-to-the-world and repositioning endpoints are:

> Brand extensions, which take an established name into a new category for the first time, such as FedEx TechConnect, a service that "configures, repairs and refurbishes" technology equipment, http://www.fedex.com/us/techconnect/, and the Starbucks Verismo coffee maker, http://www.starbucks.com/. (What about Zippo Perfume and Dr. Pepper marinade, both of which were introduced to, and withdrawn from, the market in 2012?)

- Line extensions representing different varieties of a brand, such as the Doritos flavors described above, or Pepsi Max and Diet Pepsi from Pepsi. A Cisco Consumer Packaged Goods white paper indicates that 88 percent of food and 92 percent of non-food new product introductions are line extensions (http://www.cisco.com/web/strategy/docs/retail/cisco_cpg_white_paper.pdf).

- Existing offerings that have been improved, such as Facebook allowing users to view news from applications they haven't added, http://www.facebook.com/, and Sanyo's introduction of the first-ever camera phone, http://sanyo.com/

- Reduced-price offerings, such as the $79.99 Hewlett-Packard Deskjet 3510, http://www.hp.com/#Product, and Celeron, Intel's budget alternative to Pentium, http://www.intel.com/consumer/products/processors/celeron.htm

According to Mintel, http://www.mintel.com/global-new-products-database, 41,000 new grocery products were introduced in 2012. Ongoing research by Nielsen indicates that, on average, only about 10 percent of these will be winners in the marketplace http://www.nielsen.com/us/en/newswire/2011/countdown-to-product-launch-12-key-steps.html. For results of a survey on memorable product launches, click http://www.youtube.com/watch?v=pFqVMrYSveM&feature=related.

When Walmart held its first "Get on the Shelf" contest in 2012, more than 4,000 entrants submitted videos for products ranging from household goods to children's toys, and from organic food to green items. Vying for the opportunity to be carried on Walmart.com and in the brand's U.S. retail outlets, the hopeful participants received a total of more than one million votes. Click http://brands.walmart.com/getontheshelf/ to see the winners.

Before taking an offering to market, firms can gauge its success potential through concept tests in which consumers indicate their willingness to try/buy the item based on a written description, prototype, or sample. A measure known as the "top two box score" captures the percentage of respondents who say they *definitely will buy* or *probably will buy*, as opposed to those who indicate they *might or might not buy, probably won't buy*, or *definitely won't buy*. Companies often won't launch an offering that doesn't receive a top two box of 75 percent or more.

Many grocery store chains require manufacturers to pay slotting fees or allowances in the form of cash or free cases of product before they will accept a new item. Because slotting costs can be a significant new product launch expense, manufacturers should be confident of success before attempting to secure shelf space.

Assuming that new products receive similar marketing support, what separates winners from losers? All else being equal, the goods and services that gain traction are those which create the most value for customers.

How do companies come up with ideas for enhancing consumer value? They ask customers, evaluate competitive offerings, monitor relevant improvements and innovations made in other product/service categories, look at offerings around the world, and continuously scan the business environment for changes that could have a positive or negative impact. In the end, all ideas must benefit consumers "mathematically" through subtraction or addition – by reducing the time, effort, or costs associated with use, or by enhancing sensory, psychological or experiential pleasures.

- o Would a new size appeal to consumers? 100-calorie bags introduced by Chips Ahoy!, Wheat Thins, Oreos and other snack brands created value for consumers interested in portion-control http://brands.nabisco.com/100caloriepacks/.

- o How about a different package or delivery system? Crest's neat squeeze container eliminates messy, toothpaste-filled caps http://www.crest.com/crest-products/crest-toothpastes.aspx.

- o Are consumers interested in additional flavors? Plain, peanut, almond, peanut butter, raspberry, pretzel, dark mint, and dark chocolate M&M's appeal to variety-seeking consumers http://mms.com/us/about/products/.

- o How about varying the features? Choice Hotels' Comfort Inns, Comfort Suites, Sleep and Quality Inns and Clarion Hotels each offers a different bundle of benefits to consumers, depending on the amenities they seek and the price they're willing to pay http://www.choicehotels.com/.

- o Could features of separate products/services be combined into a single offering? The BlackBerry provides email, gaming, Web browsing, photo-taking and music-downloading capabilities to its customers http://us.blackberry.com/.

o What's the main complaint consumers have about our brand? Consumers' inability to get cash when they needed it led Chemical Bank of New York to introduce the world's first, modern-day ATM http://www.chemicalbankmi.com/personal/debit_atm_cards.htm.

o Could we take something out of or add something to our current offering? Hain Pure Foods Kitchen Prescription Soups contain herbal supplements (http://www.hainpurefoods.com/), while Disney's FASTPASS eliminates waiting time at popular attractions by allowing guests to make reservations http://disneyworld.disney.go.com/guest-services/fast-pass/.

As the matrix in Chapter One shows, a great new product/service is only half of the success equation. Putting a great marketing plan behind it is the other half. It's critical that target consumers become aware of the offering, that they try and like it and, especially for consumer packaged goods, that they become repeat purchasers. *Sampling* programs are common for new products/services, because they give consumers a costless, risk-free way to try the offering. And the tactic isn't limited to passing out food products such as Pillsbury Sweet Moments Brownies at Harris Teeter. When BMW provided cars to guests of the Ritz-Carlton Hotel in Key Biscayne, FL, it was engaged in sampling.

New product/service development is particularly important in industries with short product life cycles, such as electronics and fashion goods. The concept of the product life cycle (PLC) is based on the assumption that 1) products/services have limited lifespans, 2) sales pass through distinct stages (introduction, growth, maturity and decline), each of which poses different challenges, opportunities, and problems, 3) profits rise and fall at different stages, and 4) different strategies are required in each stage.

In the introduction stage, the focus is on creating product/service awareness and establishing a market. The goal during the growth period is building brand preference and gaining market share. Intense competition during the maturity phase requires strategies designed to protect share and increase profitability. In the decline stage, new uses or features might be added in an attempt to save the product/service, or it might be discontinued.

A weakness of the PLC concept is its implicit assumption that products/services have finite lives which are independent of marketing actions. Such an assumption suggests that marketing programs and strategies should depend on the PLC stage, rather than the other way around. In fact, the PLC is a function of marketing strategies and programs. But as long as the PLC is used for descriptive, rather than predictive, purposes, it can be helpful for managers to keep the model in the backs of their minds when thinking about the health of offerings in a firm's product/service line.

The PLC is tied to the theory of diffusion of innovation, which describes the rate and rationale for the adoption of new products, practices and ideas by individuals and organizations. Innovators who are willing to pay more and/or take a risk on an unproven product are the first to enter the market, followed by early adopters, the early majority, the late majority and, finally, laggards. By the time laggards adopt, the innovation is assumed to have reached the ceiling on its market share.

Everett Rogers, a sociologist who pioneered research on the theory, found that the rate of diffusion is faster when the innovation has a significant *relative advantage* vis-à-vis existing products/services, when it exhibits a high degree of *compatibility* in terms of its ease of assimilation into an adopter's life, when it is characterized by *simplicity* rather than *complexity*, and when its *trialability* allows individuals to use or experiment with it before adoption. (A free sample of Colgate Visible White toothpaste packaged with a Colgate 360 toothbrush is an example of such an innovation.) Rogers showed that the diffusion process becomes self-sustaining at the point of critical mass, which occurs more quickly when the innovation is adopted by highly respected individuals within a social network and when positive word of mouth about the innovation's benefits creates demand among others.

Customers won't stick around for long if a brand ceases to create and deliver value for them. Continuing to market the same old products/services in the face of changing consumer preferences or changing competitive offerings is a sure recipe for revenue and profit decline. Vernon Rudolph, the late founder of Winston-Salem, NC-based Krispy Kreme Doughnuts, http://krispykreme.com/home, said that companies must "meet change with change." NPD helps keep brands fresh and customers happy and loyal.

Chapter 8: Not products, not services, but brands, brands, brands!!

The marketplace is full of products and services designed to create value by satisfying the wants and needs of consumers. Products are goods that are manufactured and can be owned; services are processes or actions that are performed and can only be experienced. Services differ from products on four key "i" dimensions: they are intangible (cannot be touched or felt), inseparable (cannot be disconnected from the provider, such as a dental hygienist or store clerk), inconsistent (cannot be standardized because delivery depends on the provider), and non-inventoriable (cannot be stored for future use or consumption).

Although we can think of products and services as falling on a continuum from pure products on one end – e.g., golf clubs – to pure services on the other – e.g., massages – in actuality most purchases involve a combination of the two – e.g., dinner at a restaurant.

Products/services – the first P of the four Ps of marketing – are a marketer's primary means of *creating value* for target consumers. They can be classified according to the type of behavior consumers exhibit in the buying process:

- *Convenience goods* such as toilet paper, frozen pizza, laundry detergent and quick-serve restaurants are frequently purchased, entail little planning or search, and are widely distributed and relatively low-priced. They are often referred to as *fast-moving consumer goods* (FMCG), *frequently purchased packaged goods* (FPPG), or *consumer packaged goods* (CPG).

- *Shopping goods* such as golf courses, cell phones, stereo equipment and cars are purchased less often, subject to more information search, and have more limited distribution.

- *Specialty goods* such as boats, luxury cars, some cruises, and designer jewelry are infrequently purchased, involve significant search, enjoy exclusive or highly selective distribution and, because of their unique features or benefits, command premium prices.

- *Credence goods* such as tax preparation, heart surgery and some auto repairs are services whose quality can't be objectively verified even after consumption/use.

- *Unsought goods* such as burial plots, personal liability insurance, and wills are often purchased as the result of adversity rather than desire.

- *Industrial goods* are sold to other businesses or to government.

All products/services deliver basic benefits to consumers. Cable TV stations entertain or inform you; cars get you from one place to another; MP3 players allow you to store, organize and play audio files; soft drinks quench your thirst. But most consumers don't buy products/services. They buy brands, which deliver value above and beyond that provided by a generic product/service.

Before we get into the topic of brands, let's review the postulates of the course. First, the fundamental objective of a firm is to maximize owner value. This can only be done if the firm is creating value for, and receiving value from, its various stakeholders: customers, employees, suppliers, channel members and support service providers. Second, companies don't make money; customers (clients, consumers, buyers, donors, patrons, or patients) give it to them. Third, marketing is the process of creating, maintaining, and improving mutually valuable customer relationships.

If customers are the source of the cash flows necessary for building owner value, then what's the basis for a firm's relationship with them? The answer is *brands*.

A brand is the liaison – the connection – between a company and its customers and, as such, is a means to an end, not an end in itself. Companies don't invest in brands for the mere sake of making the brands better; they invest in brands in order to deliver better (i.e., higher) value to customers.

There are lots of highfalutin definitions of a brand, but the simplest is this:

** A brand is a promise from the company to its customers to deliver value consistently over time. **

Think about the word "promise" and the seriousness it denotes. It's a vow. If your mother asks you to call your Great Aunt Minnie and you say you will but never actually do, you might not think it's a big deal. But if you *promise* her you will and don't, well, that's a different story. Brands pledge to deliver valuable, dependable, reliable and stable bundles of benefits, and we trust them to fulfill their pledges. Because the promises they make serve as assurances of quality and insurance policies against disappointment, brands simplify consumer decision-making. Imagine how tedious and time-consuming it would be if you had to compare the ingredients in every bottle of shampoo or cereal or sports drink on the store shelf. Isn't it much easier to always buy Pantene or Rice Krispies or Gatorade?

The most famous – and infamous – illustration of the importance of a brand (not) keeping its promise is what's alternately known as the Coke fiasco, the Coke debacle, or, less pejoratively, the New Coke launch. After more than a decade of watching Pepsi's market share climb while Coke's remained flat, after feeling the sting of Pepsi bouncing Coke out of the number one position in supermarket sales, and after taste tests demonstrated year after year that consumers preferred the sweeter taste of Pepsi to Coke, executives at the Coca-Cola Company embarked on a "if you can't beat 'em, join 'em strategy." They reformulated the iconic, flagship brand and, amid much fanfare, introduced a sweeter version to the market on April 23, 1985.

The reaction was astounding. Consumers filed class action lawsuits, attempted to buy shipments of the "old" product from overseas, placed more than 400,000 phone calls of complaint to Coca-Cola headquarters, staged public protests, launched boycotts and expressed such despair over the change that the company hired a psychiatrist to help deal with the outcry.

Stunned by consumer response, Donald Keough, Coca-Cola's then president and chief operating officer, said, "The passion for original Coke was something that just flat caught us by surprise. The simple fact is that all of the time and money and skill poured into consumer research on the new Coca-Cola could not measure or reveal the depth and emotional attachment to the original Coca-Cola felt by so many people." (http://www.time.com/time/magazine/article/0,9171,1048370-1,00.html)

Less than three months later, when the company announced the return of the original formula, ABC interrupted its daytime programming to report the momentous news. "Some cynics say that we planned the whole thing," Keough said. "The truth is, we're not that dumb, and we're not that smart."

Sugar, caramel color, caffeine and coca extract are not the stuff of which passionate attachments are made. Those ingredients are part and parcel of any cola product. Positive associations, pleasant feelings and enduring memories of Coke's roles in consumers' lives were the basis for Coke's *brand equity*, which can be thought of as the extra "bang for the buck" a marketer gains by spending money on a particular brand versus on a generic product. The strong, lasting and powerful connections consumers had with Coke were the sources of the brand's unparalleled equity. Breaking the brand's promise broke their hearts, and nearly severed Coke's relationship to the people who counted on, and loved, it.

A brand's promise answers the consumer's question, "WIFM? (What's in it for me?)" Different consumers can have different perceptions of the value delivered by the same brand. Remember that value is a subjective impression of benefits received relative to the price paid: Value = Benefits/Price.

As described in Chapter 6, benefits can be functional (performance-based), psychological (emotion-based), symbolic (principle/value-based) and experiential (sensory-based). Perceptions regarding the type and value of a brand's benefits depend on the consumer's purchase motivation and goals. A 2013 Lamborghini Veneno costs $3.9 million, yet ask an owner if the car is a good value and the answer is likely to be an emphatic "yes." It reaches 60 mph in 2.8 seconds, offers a top speed of 220 mph (both of which are functional, performance-based benefits that combine to produce an experiential benefit), and provides an almost-singular degree of exclusivity, status and prestige (value-based benefits) because only three were produced that year http://newsfeed.time.com/2013/03/05/photos-lamborghinis-new-3-9-million-veneno-supercar/.

Perceived benefits are one part of a brand's image, which consists of everything consumers know, think, believe, feel and infer about the brand, including its name, visual identity, users, and personality. Images are often the strongest points of differentiation from competitors. Objective product/service features (e.g., sugar, caramel color, caffeine and coca extract) are easy to copy; symbolic images and personalities are not. Think about ESPN vs. Spike. A Mini Cooper vs. a Ford Focus. An iPod vs. a Sansa Clip. Mtn Dew vs. Seven Up. The pairs of products/services share underlying similarities, but the brand images and personalities are very different.

To illustrate the point, let's describe two brands – Mtn Dew vs Canada Dry Ginger Ale – in the same way we might a person. In which state does it live? What kind of car does it drive? How old is it? What's its favorite TV show? If it showed up at the classroom door, in what kind of clothes would it be dressed? To what kind of music does it listen? What's the last book it read? Which college does it attend? Etc.

Although projecting human qualities or characteristics onto a brand might seem goofy, the process nevertheless demonstrates that consumers have widely divergent images of brands competing in the same product/service category. Some brands in a category appear bold and daring (Mtn Dew, perhaps); others come across as stodgy and unexciting (Seven Up, maybe). Some radiate cheerfulness (Sprite); others seem serious (Canada Dry Ginger Ale). Some are sophisticated (Schweppes Ginger Ale); others are folksy (Sierra Mist).

While consumers can have an extensive network of beliefs about a particular brand, some associations are so strongly and widely held that they constitute its core identity. For example, "chocolate" is at the heart of Hershey's image; "hot and spicy" define Tabasco; and NASCAR is heavily tied to "southern." Brand Tags, http://www.brandtags.net/, records the first thought that comes to mind when consumers see a brand name and reports responses in type size corresponding to the frequency of mention.

A brand's image is built primarily through strategies and tactics under a firm's control – STP, pricing, distribution channels, and marketing communications (advertising, publicity and public relations, consumer and trade promotion, sponsorship, cause affiliation, events, etc.). However, the image is also affected by factors outside the marketer's control, such as the type of people who buy, use and consume the brand (Coke Zero was developed for calorie-conscious males who objected to the word "diet," but just as many women drink the beverage) and types of situation in which the brand is used or consumed (Solo cups are a ubiquitous presence at fraternity parties).

In addition, the behavior of consumers can have significant consequences for a brand's image and, as a result, its marketplace and financial performance. The URL below is a link to a video produced by Domino's Pizza in response to a horrible hoax perpetrated by two (now-former) employees, or "team members" as the company refers to them http://www.youtube.com/watch?v=dem6eA7-A2I. Domino's president Patrick Doyle notes that the hoax forced the franchise owner to close his store temporarily – leading to a loss of sales – and damaged the brand.

The actions of consumers can also have dramatic positive effects on a brand. An amateur video of an unconventional wedding procession, set to the Chris Brown song "Forever," skyrocketed sales of the song to #4 on the iTunes chart and #3 on Amazon's MP3 store http://www.youtube.com/watch?v=4-94JhLEiN0.

Once a company has developed relationships with customers through its value-creating brands, it can leverage those relationships by introducing new products that bear the established brand's name.

Additional forms, flavors or varieties of the brand introduced in the current category are known as line extensions, which represent about 90 percent of all new products. *Brother vs. Brother* is a line extension of HGTV's popular remodeling show, *The Property Brothers*.

Oreo Fudge Crème Double Chocolate Fudge, Fudge Crème Coconut Delight, Golden Chocolate Crème, Fudge Crème Peanut Butter, Chocolate Banana Split Crème, Soft

Cakesters, Chocolate Birthday Cake Flavor Crème, Golden Birthday Cake Flavor Crème, Double Stuf, Go-Paks, Grab & Go, King Size, Double Stuf Heads or Tails, Fudge Crème Mint, Chocolate Berry Burst Ice Cream Flavor, Ice Cream Rainbow Shur, Bert!, Chocolate Spring, Winter Red Crème, Chocolate with Strawberry Milkshake Crème, Chocolate with Caramel Crème, Triple Double Chocolate, Football, Mint Fudge Covered, and Chocolate White Fudge Covered are just some of the Oreo Sandwich Cookie line extensions http://www.snackworks.com/search/product-results.aspx?searchText=Oreo&page=1&searchType=Product.

Wyeth Consumer Healthcare produces so many formulations of Robitussin, the company's Web site contains a feature that helps consumers pick the appropriate one http://www.robitussin.com/tools/robitussin-relief-finder.

Companies hope that new varieties will stimulate renewed interest in the brand (i.e., additional purchases!), keep consumers from switching to competitors' offerings to satisfy wants and needs, protect or expand retail shelf space, and reinforce the brand image. The problem is that brand line proliferation can confuse customers, irritate the trade, and increase the costs associated with producing and marketing so many different versions.

In some cases, the line extension represents what's referred to as a vertical, rather than a horizontal, stretch. This occurs when the brand introduces lower- or higher-priced versions of its current product/service. Tide Basic, which lacked some of the cleaning capabilities of the standard version and cost 20 percent less, was launched in the southern U.S. during the 2009 economic downturn and scrapped less than a year later. It was an example of a downward stretch, as is the Mercedes 190 that entered the market in the 1980s.

In contrast, the American Express Gold, Platinum and Centurion® cards are examples of upward stretches https://www.americanexpress.com/. The Centurion® card, named after the company's logo, is known informally as the Black card. It's made of titanium and is available by invitation-only to individuals who have had a Platinum card for at least a year and spent a minimum of $250,000 during that time period.

A concern with a lower-price-based extension is what the impact of the new version, usually targeted at an entry-level group of customers, will be on the brand's current customers. If you paid $100,000 for a prestigious Mercedes, how would you feel if a $30,000 model attracted more, and different types of, buyers to the brand? Would your perceptions of the brand's status and exclusivity remain intact? Might you switch to a different luxury brand the next time you were in the market for a car?

American Express's color designations and tiered annual fees were designed to reduce that particular risk. However, because any strategy based on price is so easy to copy, Visa and MasterCard soon followed suit with their own gold and platinum versions.

Some brands develop new brand names for stretches, such as the more expensive Lexus from Toyota, Acura from Honda, Infiniti from Nissan, and the Comfort, Quality, Clarion and Sleep Inns from Choice Hotels. In cases where the existing brand name isn't associated with a sufficient degree of quality or prestige to support a higher price, a new name helps maximize the success potential of the upward stretch. In cases of a downward stretch, a new name can protect the established brand from possible dilution and/or negative feedback effects. However, a new brand name requires higher marketing spending than is necessary with a true brand-line stretch.

Like horizontal and vertical line extensions (i.e., brand line stretches), brand extensions are new products that bear established brand names. Unlike line extensions, though, they're designed to take the brand into entirely new categories. Iams pet insurance, Starbucks coffee liqueur, the Tide to Go stain removal pen, and Oprah magazine are examples of brand extensions. Crayola pens, paints, markers and cameras are, too.

The idea behind brand extensions is that because consumers like the established brand, they'll automatically like anything and everything that bears the same name. The word "automatically" is key, because it implies that consumers won't really think about buying the brand extension, they'll just pick it up, take it to the register, and pay for it. This type of category-based, affect-driven processing (seeing the brand as being in a category by itself and basing new product/service evaluations on overall feelings about the brand) is very different from the piecemeal, cognitive-based processing associated with more involved decision-making (examining the features of the new product/service and basing evaluations on thoughtful consideration).

Because of consumers' awareness of and liking for the parent brand, brand extensions can be introduced with lower marketing budgets than those for products/services that bear new, unfamiliar brand names. However, not all brand extensions are successful or make sense. Mrs. Fields can make cookies, but not carburetors. Crest mint-flavored toothpaste is great; Crest mint chocolate candy sounds awful.

All else being equal, the best brand extensions are those that exhibit *fit* and *leverage*. Fit means that consumers would see the new product/service as logical and would expect it from the brand. Leverage means that the consumer, by knowing the brand, can think of important ways in which the extension will be different from or better than competing products/services in the new category.

The questions a marketer must ask before extending a brand are:

o   What does the brand stand for or mean in the hearts and minds of consumers?

o   In what markets and/or segments could that meaning create consumer value (the fit issue)?

o   Would the brand have a competitive advantage in those markets/segments (the leverage issue)?

o   Are the markets/segments attractive enough to warrant the required investment?

Consumer perceptions of Virgin include higher-order associations related to personality and values, including those of its founder, Sir Richard Branson http://www.virgin.com/. The brand therefore has been able to extend successfully into product/service categories completely unrelated to transportation. Virgin Mobile, Virgin Media, Virgin cosmetics and a long list of other extensions are based on the brand's image as innovative, fun, hip and high quality.

Coppertone sunglasses and Mr. Clean Car Washes have done well. CVS's Beauty 360 chain of beauty shops, Hooters energy drink, and Trump Steaks did not capture sufficient share and were withdrawn from the market. Besides the potential for failure, a risk of brand extensions is that, like stretches, they can have negative feedback effects on the brand and/or dilute the overall image.

The jury is still out on recent brand extensions such as Planter's Peanut Butter, the Jack Welch Management Institute, and LoJack's SafetyNet, a service for "tracking and rescuing people at risk of wandering." Think about other well-known brands. What could H&R Block do? Purina? Red Box? Thermos? Safelite AutoGlass? Old Spice?

In many cases, the new product isn't made by the actual owner of the brand, but instead is manufactured by a licensee who pays to use the trademark. For example, the Harley-Davidson name appears on clothing, posters, salt and pepper shakers, Christmas ornaments, boots, jewelry, bathing suits, clocks, mirrors, knives, pool tables, dog collars, barbecue grills, wallpaper borders and an almost countless number of other goods produced by companies besides Harley-Davidson. Because it's a lifestyle brand, firms believe they can make money by marketing non-motorcycle-related items that bear the iconic name – and they're willing to incur a licensing fee or royalty for the contractual right to do so.

Brands forge emotional connections with consumers and, as a result, they command price premiums, limit the negative impact of crises, enhance a firm's ability to cross cultural and international borders, offer extension opportunities, and garner wider distribution. Moreover, those with high relative levels of brand equity require less marketing spending.

Because of all these advantages, brands can have enormous economic worth. Their value can't be placed on the balance sheet and can only be captured when sold – in the form of goodwill. However, every fall Bloomberg *Businessweek* and Interbrand Corp. rank the most valuable brands in the world based on a proprietary method for estimating the earnings the names alone generate for the companies that own them.

The top 10 for 2012 are:

2012 Rank	2011 Rank	Brand name	Brand value (mms)
1	1	Coca-Cola	$77,839
2	8	Apple	$76,568
3	2	IBM	$75,532
4	4	Google	$69,726
5	3	Microsoft	$57,853
6	5	GE	$43,682
7	6	McDonald's	$40,062
8	7	Intel	$39,385
9	17	Samsung	$39,385
10	11	Toyota	$30,280

According to Interbrand, a brand's ability to generate value depends on its strength, the 10 components of which include responsiveness to market challenges and opportunities, relevance to customer needs and wants, consistency of customer experience, and differentiation from the competition. http://www.interbrand.com/en/best-global-brands/best-global-brands-methodology/Brand-Strength.aspx

High brand equity can mean more money not just for firms, but also for consumers. Bloomberg *Businessweek* reports the median cash compensation of individual graduates of the top 57 U.S. MBA schools, around graduation and after they have an average of five, 10, 15, and 20 years of work experience in the same industry. Compared to an overall 20-year average of $2.4 million, Harvard grads topped the 2012 list at $3.6 million, followed by Wharton at $3.5 million and Stanford at $3.4 million. The top brand name schools are able to attract top students, who land top positions and earn top compensation over their careers. http://images.businessweek.com/slideshows/2012-06-11/top-b-schools-for-mba-pay#slide1.

Brands are the *what* of marketing – *what* products/services will be developed to provide benefits to consumers and thereby create value for them? Brand-building begins with an understanding of consumer wants and needs and ends with . . . . Hmm, brand-building never ends, because building brands is about building relationships with the people who deliver the dollars that keep a business in business.

A brand can create relationships with new customers, and improvements to a brand's value proposition can help maintain and improve relationships with existing customers. Brands must have "something extra" (WIFM) in order to engender loyalty – and even passion – among target buyers.

Greater WIFM = greater value to customers = higher prices = higher margins = higher cash flows = more money to owners, better compensation for employees and more money to invest in brands and customers = greater WIFM and so on and so on and so on!

Keeping the brand's promise is the only way to keep the brand's customers.

Chapter 9: Price

In *Lady Windemere's Fan*, a 19th Century play by Oscar Wilde, Lord Darlington delivers a line that might well have been spoken by a marketing professor in the classroom today. "What is a cynic?" he asks rhetorically. "A man who knows the price of everything and the value of nothing."

Price, the third of the four Ps, has a unique role in the marketing mix because it not only helps create value for customers, but also *captures value* for the firm. Three of the Ps – product, place and promotion – consume company resources in the process of value creation. Developing and producing goods and services, establishing appropriate distribution channels, and reaching and communicating with the target market require significant financial investments. A company's pricing strategy is designed to harvest the fruits of these activities by delivering a positive return on the expenditures and providing sufficient margin to allow earnings for owners and continuing investment in customers.

Price affects profits in three different ways, reflected in the equations below: directly through revenue; indirectly through quantity sold, which naturally is influenced by price; and indirectly through total costs, which decrease as a company's production experience or volume increase. The cost-reducing impact of greater production history is known as an experience- or learning-curve effect, while the cost-reducing impact of greater volume is referred to as economies of scale.

Profit = Total Revenue – Total Costs

Total Revenue = Price x Quantity

Price x Quantity = Price per unit sold x # units sold

Let's go back to your lemonade stand, a one-product "firm." The lemonade you sell has to cover your initial investment of $25, pay for additional ingredients and supplies, and still leave enough money for your piggybank or your snowboard. If you can't meet your operating expenses or earn enough profit to make it worthwhile for you to get up early on Saturday mornings, your days as a liquid refreshments entrepreneur will end! Obviously, setting the right price for your brand is essential.

The financial success or failure of a large company with many offerings does not rest on a single brand. Nevertheless, each and every good or service sold should contribute its fair share to ongoing operations to avoid being a drain on resources and a drag on profits.

What does Lord Darlington have to do with any of this? Although Wilde's play is about morality and marriage, his character unwittingly acknowledges a marketing truth: Price and value are connected, but are not the same concepts.

The equation introduced earlier shows the relationship between the two:

Value = Benefits/Price

From a purely mathematical standpoint, value increases when:

- o More benefits are offered at the current (i.e., same) price
  - Tide improved the whitening power of its laundry detergent

- o The same benefits are offered at a lower price
  - Volvo announced price cuts on several of its 2013 models

- o More benefits are offered at a lower price
  - Three months after Apple's iPad introduction, Amazon enhanced the contrast on its Kindle screen, increased the darkness of fonts, and gave the product a graphite finish – while lowering the price by more than $150

Value remains constant when more benefits are offered at a higher price (e.g., more options on a car), or fewer benefits are offered at a lower price (e.g., a basic version of a car).

However, another important relationship between price and value isn't intuitively obvious when looking at the equation. From the standpoint of consumers, a higher price can be considered a benefit and, consequently, be associated with higher perceived value. For example, individuals who desire exclusivity believe that more expensive items offer them greater prestige and status. Moreover, a brain-scanning study by Cal Tech and Stanford investigators showed that price can even affect a consumer's actual enjoyment of a consumption experience. Researchers had subjects taste wine that was priced at either $5 versus $45, or at $10 versus $90. Despite the fact that it was exactly the same cabernet, MRIs showed that when sipping the higher priced wines, more blood and oxygen were sent to the brain's pleasure center (http://news.cnet.com/8301-13580_3-9849949-39.html).

In the 1866 short story "The Accursed House" by French author Emile Gaboriau, the protagonist inherits an apartment building from his uncle and, believing the rents to be exhorbitant orders the protesting concierge to reduce them by one-third. The 23 tenants, some of whom had lived in the building for more than 40 years and most of whom had never even spoken to one another, immediately gathered together to speculate as to the reason for such extraordinary behavior. By the end of one week, everyone had moved out, certain that an impending catastrophe was behind the unheard-of reduction.

When Amazon bought 440,000 digital copies of Lady Gaga's "Born This Way" album in May 2011 and sold them for $0.99, the release dropped from #1 to #8 on the pop charts and to #20 on iTunes. Music critics and fans across the Internet decried Amazon's move, which they said "devalued" the singer's brand in particular and music in general.

Consumers – real and fictional – often rely on price as a predictor of quality and often overestimate the strength of the relationship. They believe the adage that "you get what you pay for" and, as a result, their quality inferences can influence actual purchase decisions. Consequently, marketers must be very careful not to overlook the effect of price on value through its impact on perceived quality (i.e., benefits).

Many marketers make an even more fundamental mistake. They use cost-plus pricing, which entails adding a standard markup – for example, 20 percent – to a product's or service's cost of goods sold. This method ignores the value consumers receive from the offering and leaves money in buyers' purses or pockets that they would willingly give up.

Suppose you were in charge of pricing a new line of cards by American Greetings that includes pre-stamped mailing envelopes. Would you simply add 46 cents (the current cost of a first-class stamp) to the card's price? If that were your strategy, you'd be disregarding important factors related to the company and its customers. For example, how much did American Greetings spend to come up with the idea? What was the expense associated with testing and evaluating various stamp-imprinting processes? How much will the ink required for imprinting add to the cost of goods sold? Will additional employees be needed to deal with record-keeping and accounting functions related to the innovation? What about the cost of pre-stamped envelopes damaged by consumer handling in retail stores? How much is the savings of time, energy and gasoline worth to customers who otherwise would have to travel to stores or post offices to purchase stamps? If the pre-stamped envelopes allow senders to mail cards sooner and therefore avoid missing recipients' birthdays or other special occasions, how much would buyers be willing to pay for that psychological benefit? Clearly, 46 cents doesn't cover the costs of the innovation to American Greetings or capture the value consumers receive from it.

The right price reflects a match between a firm's beliefs about the value created by its brand relative to other relevant offerings and the right customer's perceptions of the value gained from that brand relative to other relevant offerings. Perceptions are affected by:

- Availability of substitutes
  - If your vehicle could run on distilled water or Kool-Aid, you would probably buy something other than gasoline when fuel costs rose.

- Competition
  - Except under the most unusual of circumstances, you wouldn't pay $4.99 per gallon for gas at Texaco if the price at Shell, Exxon, and BP were $3.29.

- Use
  - A 12-ounce container of 16 parts gas premixed with one part oil for use in two-cycle engines (e.g., some chain saws, lawnmowers and go-karts) is about $5, or more than $26 per gallon.

- Users
  - NASCAR pays more than $9.70 for a gallon of Sunoco 260 GTX

- Value in use
  - $50 for two gallons of gasoline would be outrageous . . . unless your tank was empty and you needed to make a flight to the World Cup.

- Bundling
  - If a car dealer adds $100 to the sticker price of a new car sold with a full tank of gas, you might not even notice, let alone care.

In addition to being too cost-oriented, prices set by marketers are often too static and not revised to capitalize on market changes; set independently from the marketing mix rather than as intrinsic element of strategy; and not varied enough for different products/services, segments, distribution channels, or purchase occasions.

Pricing decisions should be made with input from sales, production, finance, and accounting. When setting price, marketers should start with the objective, which can include:

- Survival, such as when the industry is marked by overcapacity, intense competition, or changing customer preferences. The firm stays in business as long as revenue covers costs.

- Maximize current profits (i.e., maximum profits, cash flow and return on investment). Firms use what's known as a *skimming* price when they have patents or other barriers to entry, such as an exclusive image; when there are a sufficient number of buyers with high demand; when they reach the market far ahead of competitors; and when the unit costs of small volume are not so high that the advantage is canceled out.

- Maximize market share. A *penetration* price makes sense when low price discourages competition; when higher volume leads to lower production and distribution costs through experience curve effects; and in a price-sensitive market where low prices stimulate growth.

According to Nagle and Holden in *Strategy and Tactics of Pricing*, consumers are less price-sensitive when:
  - The brand is more distinctive
  - Buyers are less aware of substitutes and can't compare their quality
  - The expenditure is small compared to the end benefit, or is a smaller part of the buyer's total income
  - Part of the cost is borne by another party
  - The brand is perceived to have more quality, prestige, or exclusivity

Despite the fact that brands typically are distinctive and have high-quality images, marketers nevertheless are often all too eager to engage in discounting as a means of boosting sales. They treat price as a tactical tool for responding to competitor actions, rather than as a strategic component of a marketing plan designed to create, maintain and improve customer relationships.

When marketing is done right, it increases margins. Overuse of price-cutting gives away margin and *amounts to paying consumers to like the brand.* Besides, in addition to being the easiest decision variable to change, price is also the easiest to copy. For example, when Delta announces a fare reduction on popular routes, American, US Airways and United usually soon follow. For this reason, price can rarely serve as the basis for a sustainable competitive advantage.

Price is related to two fundamental concepts in economics, supply and demand. Demand refers to how much of a product/service consumers will buy at a given price, while supply refers to how much of a product/service producers will offer at a given price.

Most goods and services are presumed to have downward-sloping demand curves, meaning demand decreases as price increases. For example, the Congressional Budget Office estimates that a 10 percent increase in the price of a gallon of gas will reduce consumption four percent www.cbo.gov/ftpdocs/88xx/doc8893/01-14-GasolinePrices.pdf.

The supply curve, on the other hand, is presumed to be upward-sloping, meaning less volume is produced at lower selling prices. Latin American farmers cut their organic coffee bean output when lower prices left them unable to justify the higher costs and smaller yields http://www.csmonitor.com/World/Americas/2010/0103/Organic-coffee-Why-Latin-America-s-farmers-are-abandoning-it.

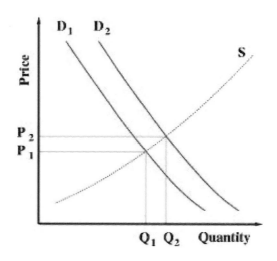

The degree to which a change in price leads to a change in demand is known as *elasticity*. If the ratio of the percentage change in quantity sold to the percentage change in price is greater than 1 (i.e., $\partial q/\partial p > 1$), the product/service is said to have *elastic* demand. For example, if the price of a movie rental goes up 20 percent and demand goes down 30 percent, the demand elasticity would be 1.5.

If the ratio of the percentage change in quantity sold to the percentage change in price is less than 1, the product/service has *inelastic* demand. For example, if toilet paper prices rise 20 percent and demand falls one percent, demand elasticity would be .05.

Elasticity can be highly situation-based. You might be unwilling to pay $12 for sunscreen at your corner Walgreen's, but if you're about to embark on an eight-hour deep-sea fishing expedition off the coast of Key West, you might buy a bottle from a dockside shop without thinking twice.

Sales and discounts are based on marketers' beliefs that demand is elastic and that a temporary price reduction will increase purchases enough to cover the lost margin. Let's look at the financial implications of a commonly used discount tool – a $0.50 coupon – and apply it to an ordinary toothbrush:

Price at which manufacturer sells to retailer (assumed)	$ 1.00
Manufacturer's cost of goods sold per toothbrush (assumed)	.35
Manufacturer's margin before coupon	$ 0.65
Cost to manufacturer of each coupon redeemed at retailer	.50
Manufacturer's margin after coupon	$ 0.15
# of toothbrushes sold (assumed)	1,000
Manufacturer's total gross margin before coupon	$6,500
Manufacturer's total gross margin after coupon	$1,500
"Lost" margin due to coupon promotion	$5,000
Increase in sales required to cover cost of coupon promotion	333%

When was the last time a $0.50 coupon on a toothbrush prompted you to run out and buy *one*, let alone the *3 1/3rd* required for the manufacturer to equal the revenue earned without the promotion? Yet according to the NCH Coupon Facts Report, in 2012 marketers distributed 305 billion coupons worth an average of $1.53 apiece https://www2.nchmarketing.com/ResourceCenter/assets/0/22/28/76/226/457/735949da63a14 f209014dd04c27f1472.pdf.

In effect, a brand's price signals the selling firm's belief of what the brand is worth to the target market. If consumers require a discount before they're willing to purchase, the seller either overestimated the value or conditioned buyers to wait for a sale. Sales draw consumers' focus away from an offering's value toward its price. Consumer sales promotions can play an important role in an integrated marketing communications program, but those that are discount-based must be used judiciously and infrequently.

What about the effect of price *increases* on sales? Lower elasticity is typically seen when few substitutes are available, few competitors exist, buyers don't readily notice the higher price, buyers are slow to change their purchase habits, and buyers think the higher price is justified. Those conditions are most likely to pertain to strong brands. The greater the value created by a brand, the less sensitive its target customers are to price hikes.

When establishing price, demand sets a ceiling on price and costs set the floor. Unfortunately, as previously noted, marketers often use cost-plus pricing, which entails adding a fixed percentage, or markup, to costs. Others set a price that will deliver a target return on investment (ROI) established by the company. Still others essentially copy competitor prices. None of these methods take into account the value the brand creates for consumers, which should be the basis for pricing strategy.

Consumer assessments of value depend upon their reference points. The Internet makes it easy to search for and evaluate prices. Do consumers compare a brand's price to competitor prices? To past prices? To the price of functional substitutes, e.g., the cost of renting a movie for Friday night entertainment versus bowling? These are questions for which marketers should have answers before making price decisions.

Once a price is established, a company must decide whether and when to adapt it:

- *Geographical* pricing occurs when marketers take into account variations in costs or consumers by area or region. Walmart, for example, follows a local area pricing strategy whereby items are priced lower when there is nearby competition, such as a Target store, than when there isn't. B2B companies have to decide whether distant customers should be charged higher prices to cover higher shipping costs or lower prices to win additional business.

- *Countertrade* is sometimes used when buyers lack sufficient hard currency to pay for purchases. When Pepsi first entered the former Soviet Union, it exchanged syrup for Stolichnaya vodka, which it then marketed in the U.S. The company later accepted a fleet of 20 naval vessels that it sold for scrap steel to pay for Pepsi products being distributed in the country. Avon representatives in Brazil – the company's second-largest market behind the U.S. – ,kayak down the Amazon River to visit customers and accept payment in gold nuggets, chickens and wood.

- With *discriminatory* pricing, which is not only legal but also good business, a company charges different prices based on such factors as:
  - Volume
    - Thorlo over-the-calf thin cushion men's dress socks are $16.99 a pair, or a pack of six for $95.94, which is a savings of $1 per pair
  - Customer segment
    - At many movie theaters, children and seniors pay less to see The Croods than you do
  - Product form
    - A travel-size container of Irish Spring body wash carries a higher price per ounce than a standard container
  - Image
    - A limited edition designer bottle of ck One perfume is more expensive than a regular bottle
  - Distribution channel
    - A bag of Lay's potato chips in a vending machine costs more than the same bag in a grocery store
  - Location
    - Parterre box seats for the Metropolitan Opera premiere of *La Cenerentola* are $1,197 apiece, while those in the balcony are $102
  - Time
    - Student tickets to see Ed Burns at the 2013 Reynolda Film Festival at Wake Forest University were free in advance, or $5 at the door

- o Situation
    - A Kodak single-use camera is $6 at CVS Pharmacy, but $9.99 at DisneyWorld

- *Promotional* pricing includes coupons, rebates, low-interest financing, longer payment terms, free/low-cost warranties or service contracts, discounts and sales.

Companies with lines of complementary or substitutable offerings typically use *product mix* pricing. Intel's Pentium chip is more expensive than its lower-tier Celeron. H-P printers are relatively inexpensive, but the company's ink cartridges are not. Verizon offers two-part calling plans that include a fixed monthly fee plus a per-minute charge. Ordering a cable TV, high-speed Internet and digital phone bundle of services from Time-Warner Cable is cheaper for consumers than subscribing to those services from separate providers. The list price on a Lexus 450 RX with all-wheel drive is higher than on a model without that option.

If it wasn't apparent to you before, it should be now: A company's top-line revenue and bottom-line profits depend on the prices it charges customers for the value created for them by brands. The price tag on a pair of Ray-Ban sunglasses or Miu Miu platform shoes may seem like "just a number" to the average consumer, but it was – or should have been! – the result of careful thought and consideration by marketers.

Notice the word "brand" in the paragraph above. A layer of air-laid paper and superabsorbent polymers sandwiched between an outer shell of breathable polyethylene film and an inner band of nonwoven material describes a generic disposable diaper available at $39.99 for 252, or about $0.16 a diaper. The same contents embellished with stripes, ruffles, madras print or one of eight other special styles by designer Cynthia Rowley is a Pampers brand disposable diaper that sells at $14.99 for a 24-pack, or about $0.62 a diaper. Pampers is the number one brand worldwide, suggesting that parents value appearance as well as performance . . . *and are willing to pay almost 288 percent more for the additional benefit!*

Bergdorf Goodman sells Scott Sternberg's Band of Outsiders cotton gabardine khakis for $550. Is that too much? You might think so, but it's the target market's opinion that matters, not yours.

All else being equal, higher prices allow higher margins. And as noted in the introductory chapter, higher margins aren't about being greedy. Higher margins mean more money to invest in customers in the form of research on new product/service development, improvements to current products/services, enhanced customer experiences at retail and online, upgraded customer service, etc. Higher margins also mean more money to invest in better compensation and improved working conditions for employees, streamlined supply chain relationships, advanced production processes and equipment, and support for communities and causes.

Firms mustn't leave money on the table that buyers are willing to give them – money that's needed to finance ongoing investment in consumers' future happiness . . . and the company's future cash flows.

Chapter 10: Distribution channels

Brands and the ways in which they are priced and promoted create value for consumers. Almost.

In point of fact, brands create only the *potential* for value. A fantastic new canipulator (?!) that's never released from the manufacturing facility might make the company very proud, but it won't improve the lives of target consumers unless it's made available for purchase somewhere.

Place, the third P of the four Ps, refers to a company's distribution channels and is responsible for *delivering value* to the target market.

The distribution channel is a part of a firm's overall supply chain, which consists of the entire network of partners involved in the value-delivery process – from the suppliers of raw materials to the retailers who sell finished goods and services to consumers. Let's use organic clothing as an example. The supply chain for the Alternative Apparel brand (http://alternativeapparel.com/) might include organic cotton growers who supply the raw cotton, textile mills who process the cotton, trucking and rail services who transport the raw materials and the finished goods to and from the mills and the manufacturer, inventory warehousing firms who store the raw materials and/or finished goods, the Alternative Apparel manufacturing company itself, and retailers such as Dillard's and Piperlime who sell the apparel to consumers.

The organization, coordination and integration of a firm's supply chain partners and processes are known collectively as supply chain management. This cross-disciplinary function is responsible for the sourcing, acquisition, storage, transportation and conversion of raw inputs (i.e., materials and supplies) into consumer outputs (i.e., finished goods and services). The goal of supply chain management is to minimize costs and maximize end-to-end performance so that consumers can receive the highest possible value.

How is that value transmitted from producers of goods and services to consumers of those goods and services? Through the distribution channel.

Suppose that, without any doubt whatsoever, you figured out the meaning of existence. You believe your realization can change people's lives for the better, so you write a book to let everyone in on your secret. How should you distribute the book to consumers you think would value knowing "the answer"?

You could open a mall kiosk and sell copies to passersby. Or you could let customers order it from your Web site and/or from Amazon. If you're lucky, Barnes and Noble will sell it online *and* in its retail stores. You could try to talk Starbucks into carrying the book in its coffee shops, alongside Starbucks Entertainment. Or you could distribute it through health food stores. You could also set up a sales table at a Star Trek convention. If you're really energetic and motivated, you could sell door-to-door in neighborhoods in your hometown.

How do you choose the best approach? Your objective should be to make the book available to consumers where they want it, when they want it, in the quantities they want. That's what *place* decisions are all about.

As the word is used in the field, *place* pertains not only to the location at which consumers purchase a product/service, but also to a product's/service's entire channel of distribution. The channel consists of the intermediaries, if any, between the manufacturer/producer and end customers – brokers who connect manufacturers to wholesalers and/or retailers; wholesalers who buy in bulk from manufacturers and distribute to retailers; and retailers who sell to consumers such as you.

Intermediaries are useful because *manufacturers produce large quantities of a limited variety of products/services, while consumers want limited quantities of a wide variety of products/services.*

Apple sold five million iPhone 5s in a single weekend in September 2012, and Microsoft's total worldwide sales of the Xbox 360 game consoles exceed 76 million, but you only want one of each item – if any. You also want, at most, one Nike+ iPod Sport Kit, one Toshiba SDP93S portable DVD player, one Dell Inspiron Mini 10 notebook computer, and one Sony Bravia Z5800 HDTV. Best Buy, a consumer electronics retailer, makes shopping for these brands convenient for you.

Channel members create value for manufacturers and consumers by serving three different types of functions. The first is *transactional* – they buy products from manufacturers, sell them to consumers, and assume risk. The second is *logistical* – they put together products from a variety of manufacturers, carry inventory, break cases and other large quantities into smaller amounts, and transport products. The third is *facilitative* – they finance, inspect and market products.

Now that you know the benefits that can be provided by channel members, let's go back to the example of the book you wrote. How will you determine your distribution strategy? In general, producers must consider three primary criteria:

1.) Extent of distribution coverage desired
   o Intensive: many retailers
      ▪ Common with *convenience* goods that are low-priced, low-risk and frequently purchased: soda, laundry detergent, bread and milk
   o Selective: a few retailers
      ▪ Used for *shopping* goods that might involve pre-sale advice/information and post-sale service: clothing, TVs, home furnishings and jewelry
   o Exclusive: one or two retailers in a specified geographic area
      ▪ Used with *specialty* goods that are high-priced, infrequently purchased and require personal selling: automobiles, boats, and some brands of watches
2.) Ability to satisfy needs and wants of target market
   • In terms of convenience, availability, and sales support
3.) Profitability
   o Allow adequate margin and sales volume

The shortest distribution channel exists when companies sell directly to consumers, avoiding intermediaries. This direct-to-consumer strategy is used when production volume is low and demand must therefore be limited, or when the firm wants tighter control over the brand image and the customer experience, or when the target market is highly focused and small in size. Williams-Sonoma, http://www.williams-sonoma.com/, Horchow, http://www.horchow.com/, and Garrett Popcorn, http://www.garrettpopcorn.com/, all market directly through their own stores, catalogs, the Internet, or a combination of the three.

A longer distribution channel is characteristic of companies with narrow product lines and insufficient volume to justify the cost of transporting goods from the manufacturing plant to retailers, or with products whose retailers are geographically dispersed. McCormick doesn't produce enough spices, extracts, flavors, and oils to make it cost-efficient to sell and deliver directly to retailers. Consequently, it sells to wholesalers, who distribute products from a number of different manufacturers to retailers.

In between are brands such as Crest toothpaste. You can't buy Crest directly from Procter & Gamble, the manufacturer, because selling one or two tubes at a time to the brand's millions of customers around the world would be cost-prohibitive for the company and for you. Instead, you can conveniently buy the brand from a drugstore such as CVS, supermarket such as Safeway, mass marketer such as Walmart, convenience store such as Stop 'n' Go, or buying club such as Costco. Each of these retailers who sells to consumers is a member of Crest's distribution channel. P&G's portfolio includes beauty and grooming and household care products. Gillette, Old Spice, Olay, Ivory, Braun, Scope, Crest, Tide, Dawn, Bounce, and Febreze are just a few of the P&G brands with which you're probably familiar. Because the company sells such high volumes of so many different products, it's cost-efficient to deliver cases of its frequently purchased packaged goods by truck directly to food, drug and mass merchandising retailers http://www.pg.com/en_US/index.shtml.

Some brands adopt a hybrid system. Starbucks uses a direct retailing system to sell to consumers in its own retail stores, a direct marketing system to sell to consumers over the Internet, and an indirect retailing system to sell to consumers through grocery stores.

What kind of distribution strategy will you choose for your book?

Most consumer products and services are purchased from retailers. The #1 company on the Fortune 500 is Walmart, which operates 4,049 stores in the U.S., an additional 6,222 in overseas markets, and had revenues of more than $469 billion in 2012.

The retail locations at which a brand is sold should both reflect and reinforce its image. Apple announced in November, 2009, that it would open 40 to 50 new retail sites in 2010 and would focus on what Ron Johnson, then the company's senior vice president of retailing, called "significant stores." (Johnson was hired as JCPenney's CEO in late 2011 and fired in mid-2013.) Apple coined a new term to describe its retailing approach. Other more common terms used to describe bricks-and-mortar establishments and online sellers are:

- Mom-and-Pop – small, individually owned and operated; cater to the local community with a high level of service but relatively small product selection.

- Mass merchandisers – general or specialty stores that offer discount pricing, relatively few services, and comparatively lower-quality products.

- Warehouse stores – mass discounters that offer lower prices than traditional mass merchandisers; often require buyers to make purchases in large quantities; provide few services and limited product selection; may require customers to purchase memberships in order to gain access.

- Category killers – large specialty stores that carry huge numbers of brands within fairly narrow product lines, such as electronics (e.g., Best Buy), office supplies (e.g., Staples) and sporting goods (e.g., Sports Authority).

- Department stores – general merchandisers offering reasonably high levels of service.

- Boutiques – small stores carrying very specialized and often high-end merchandise.

- Variety stores – so-called "dollar stores" offering a relatively small selection of low-cost goods.

- E-tailers – online retailers who can be one of the types above.

Vending machines represent another approach to retailing. "Automated retail kiosks" have long been associated with soft drinks and candy, but more recently have been used to dispense a wide array of products, including iPods, rental movies, shoes, baby bottles, diapers and gold nuggets. Some of the most unusual vending machines around the world can be found in Japan, where high population density and limited retail space make them a convenient, cost-effective means of reaching consumers. A drink-dispensing unit introduced in Tokyo in 2010 uses facial recognition technology to make beverage recommendations http://www.telegraph.co.uk/news/worldnews/asia/japan/8136743/Japanese-vending-machine-tells-you-what-you-should-drink.html.

Let's say you've reached a decision regarding the distribution channel for your book. You want to sell at Starbuck's because you believe the company's patrons represent your target market. Will Starbuck's simply open its doors and invite you to "come on in"? Of course not. The deal has to be in the firm's interest, too.

Because retailers have a finite amount of space in which to stock an almost infinite number of items (for example, a typical chain grocery store stocks 60,000 different SKUs), they must carry an assortment that not only meets consumer needs and wants, but also maximizes cash flows. Two important metrics are *sales per square foot*, which captures the average revenue produced for every square foot of selling space, and *inventory turnover* ($ sales/$ inventory), which reflects how many times the stock is sold and replaced in a given time period. To depict the best way to display products in order to maximize both measures, retailers of fast-moving consumer goods often use *planograms*. Planograms are illustrations that show how products should be merchandised, i.e., in what quantity and in which area/on which shelf they should be stocked.

Best Buy announced in 2011 that it would lease space in its stores to local grocers, beauty-supply brands and home-furnishings firms. Online competition, including from its own brand, was behind efforts to reduce its retail footprint by as much as 20 percent and thereby increase the inventory turnover and sales/square foot of remaining floor space.

In August 2010, *Forbes* published a ranking of the 10 most trustworthy retailers based on a 100-factor assessment of the quality of their accounting and management practices. Mass merchandise chains and department stores were notably absent from the list, which was filled with specialty retail chains such as Hot Topic in the number one spot, followed by Citi Trends, Havertys and Fred's http://www.forbes.com/2010/08/16/most-trustworthy-retailers-personal-finance-best-retailers.html?boxes=Homepagechannels.

Interbrand ranks the most valuable retail brands in the U.S. (#1 is Walmart), Canada (#1 is lululemon athletica), China (#1 is Suning), the U.K. (#1 is Tesco), Japan (#1 is Uniqlo) and several other countries. To be considered, a brand has to generate at least 50 percent of sales through its branded retail locations (e.g., Apple doesn't qualify). Value is determined through a proprietary method that considers the brand's financial performance, role in consumer purchase decisions, and ability to deliver expected future earnings http://www.interbrand.com/en/BestRetailBrands/2013/Best-Retail-Brands-Brand-View.aspx.

The National Retail Foundation's Stores, http://www.stores.org/, lists the Top 100 U.S. retailers by revenue (#1 is Walmart), Top 250 Global (#1 is Walmart), Hot 100 fastest-growing retail chains (#1 is Sprouts Farmer's Market), and the Favorite 50 online retailers based on consumer survey results (#1 is Amazon).

Forrester Research predicts that U.S. online retail sales will reach $370 billion in 2017, up from $230 billion in 2013, while in Europe the number will rise over the same period from $165 billion to $247 billion. Forrester also estimates that by 2014, 53 percent of all retail sales, or $1.4 trillion, will be online transactions or influenced by Web research.

Retailers have brand images that are influenced by, but also separate from, the images of the brands they sell. Could Neiman Marcus sell Crocs? Of course it could, but the question is *should,* not *could.* Crocs don't fit with the retailer's exclusive, high-end image. If Crocs introduced a line studded with Swarovski crystals, perhaps the brand could get its foot (or shoe!) in Neiman Marcus' door.

When developing marketing strategies, retailers must consider store location, types and quantities of merchandise to carry, physical appearance and atmosphere of the store, level and type of customer service to offer, means of communication with customers, and promotion policy. All of these decisions should depend on the needs and wants of the target market. If the retailer isn't delivering value to customers, it could end up like Circuit City, Sharper Image, or Linens 'n' Things – all of which closed their doors in the 2000s.

There's simply no *place* in today's competitive retail landscape for store brands that don't stand out in the hearts and minds of consumers!

Chapter 11: Integrated marketing communications

A value-creating product/service (a brand!) that is appropriately priced and distributed in the most appropriate places (the first 3 Ps) cannot be successful in the market unless consumers are aware of the brand and the benefits it offers.

Promotion, more commonly referred to as integrated marketing communications (IMC), is the fourth of the four Ps and is responsible for *communicating value* to target customers. The word "integrated" denotes that all planned contacts with consumers are managed in such a way as to deliver a *clear, cogent, consistent message and image.*

As an illustration, consider the 2007 campaign by the United States Marine Corps to recruit 39,028 quality young men and women necessary to sustain Congress' expected level of readiness. The Corps launched an integrated marketing communications campaign that included commercials on sports and entertainment TV programs; public service announcements on TV, radio, outdoor, and online media; an in-school presence with posters, broadcast ads on ChannelOne, and print ads in school magazines; movie theater advertising; online banner ads, rich media, and search-engine optimization; a Web site (http://www.marines.com/); six direct mailings to high school juniors and seniors; event marketing and sponsorship; and recruiter support in the form of brochures, collateral material, posters, and educational films and videos.

The look, feel and tone of each component were consistent with the Corps' image as an elite, tough organization meant only for individuals with tremendous strength of mind, body and spirit. The result? Mission accomplished! The Marines exceeded their recruiting goals and met or surpassed objectives related to the target market's attitudes, beliefs, and perceptions. In addition, the campaign received an Effie Award, established by the American Marketing Association to recognize the most effective advertising worldwide each year.

Colgate introduced its Max Fresh Burst oral care youth brand to the Hispanic market with an IMC campaign (http://www.youtube.com/watch?v=5B4rDPnB1sA) that included commercials on "Bailando," the top-rated TV show among 1st- and 2nd-generation Hispanics; sponsorship of the Latin Billboard Music Awards; print ads in top Hispanic publications; a Website; a ringtone promotion at events and retail locations; and street festivals in Los Angeles and New York City. The campaign featured Tito El Bambino, a reggaeton star, who encouraged the target market to "abre tu boca, ya te toca" (open your mouth, your time is now).

The first step in developing an IMC program is to *identify the relevant target audience.* For example, although virtually everyone, everywhere is in Coca-Cola's overall target market, creating and delivering messages with an equally positive impact on each individual customer is impossible. Consequently, Coke regularly designs campaigns to reach smaller consumer subsets. In 2009, the brand ran a promotion designed to help Hispanic adults learn English. Through a partnership with the developer of the video-based language program Inglés sin Barreras (English without Borders), Coke gave consumers opportunities to obtain English-Spanish mini-dictionaries and DVD lessons. That same year Coke also launched Secret Formula, a component of the Open Happiness/Destapa La Felicidad campaign, to establish a dialogue with Hispanic and other teens.

Once the target audience has been set, marketers should then *determine appropriate marketing communications objectives*. For a new brand, these include creating awareness and generating trial. For a growing brand, the goals might be increasing the repurchase rate, building preference, stimulating word-of-mouth and inducing consumers to switch from a competitor. A mature brand is likely to focus on protecting shelf space, maintaining distribution channels, and preserving sales. Other objectives include informing, educating, reminding, rewarding, gaining retail support, repositioning, encouraging multiple purchases, reinforcing brand personality and image . . . .

After the target market and objectives have been determined, the marketer must *set the marketing communications budget*. In reality, marketers often are told how much they can spend first and then allocate the total across target audiences and media. However, common practice is not always best practice!

Marketers budget significant amounts of money for marketing communications. As the June 2013 *Advertising Age* figures in the table below show, the top global spender in 2012 was Procter & Gamble, the world's largest consumer products manufacturer. The company allocated more than $13 million *a day* (= $4.83 billion/365 days per year) to reaching consumers – $5 million more *each day* than the next largest spender, GM.

2012 Rank	Company	Measured Media
1	Procter & Gamble	$4.83 billion
2	General Motors Co.	$3.07 billion
3	Comcast	$2.99 billion
4	AT&T	$2.91 billion
5	Verizon Communications	$2.38 billion
6	Ford Motor Co.	$2.28 billion
7	L'Oreal	$2.24 billion
8	JPMorgan Chase & Co.	$2.09 billion
9	American Express	$2.07 billion
10	Toyota Motor Corp.	$2.01 billion

The final step in the planning process is *development of the actual communications plan*. What marketing communications components should be included in order to achieve the desired objectives? What message will be conveyed? What are the best media for delivering the message/reaching the target audience? In short, the marketer must decide *what* to say, *to whom*, by *what means*, and *how often*.

When developing a plan, marketers often consider the *gross ratings points* (GRPs) associated with different options. GRPs are a function of the level of *reach* (the percent of people in the target market who are exposed to a message at least once) multiplied by *frequency* (the number of times they are exposed). GRPs = reach x frequency.

Some *media* (e.g., TV or radio or print publications) and media *vehicles* (i.e., specific broadcast programs, or publications, such as American Idol or ESPN Sports Center; or The Rush Limbaugh Show or Car Talk; or *Sports Illustrated* or *National Geographic*) have audiences/readerships that can be measured and that expose the message to large numbers of people each time it is seen, heard, or read.

All else being equal, greater exposure (i.e., wider *reach*) means higher costs. For example, Super Bowl XLVI in February 2012 between the victorious New York Giants and the New England Patriots *reached* more than 111 million viewers, making it the most-watched single TV program ever. The 2013 game between the winning Baltimore Ravens and the San Francisco 49ers game had an audience of 108.4 million. The consistently huge viewership is one of the reasons advertisers pay dearly for commercial time: a 30-second spot during the 2013 match-up cost $4 million. That covered a single airing only (i.e., a *frequency* of one), and didn't include casting, production, editing or other expenses! Anheuser-Busch narrowly beat out Tide in *USA Today's* Ad Meter poll with a heart-warming spot in which a horse and its trainer are reunited. You can check out the results at http://admeter.usatoday.com/articles/view/the-results. The best-ever Super Bowl ad is widely considered to be a 1984 spot for the Apple MacIntosh (http://adage.com/superbowl/top20).

A single exposure to a message is rarely enough to produce the desired effect on the target market. Consumers might see or hear an ad several times before paying attention to it, a few more times before thinking about it, and a couple more times before deciding to try or buy the advertised brand.

Media planning is a very specialized area of marketing communications, and a more detailed explanation of the concept is beyond the scope of this textbook. Suffice is to say that, given a fixed budget, a marketer generally must trade off wider reach for lower frequency, and higher frequency for narrower reach.

The push and pull of IMC

There are two basic approaches to marketing communications, and they are referred to as *push* and *pull*.

Push encompasses tactics that typically are designed to achieve short-run sales objectives, such as increasing units sold, boosting trial, accelerating purchases, or stimulating brand switching. When the tactics are aimed at channel intermediaries – wholesalers and retailers known collectively as the *trade* – they are called trade promotions. Such promotions aim to create a win-win situation for all parties because the trade receives an incentive from the manufacturer to order more of the brand and promote it to end users, i.e., *to build sales and to do it now*. Examples of trade promotions include volume discounts, point-of-purchase displays, promotional cash allowances, in-store product demonstrations, "spiffs" (commissions or bonuses based on performance), product sampling, cooperative advertising programs, trade journal advertising, sales contests and trade shows.

The High Point Market is the largest furnishings industry trade show in the world. Closed to the public, the Market brings more than 85,000 retailers, decorators and wholesale buyers to High Point, NC, twice a year to view offerings from 2,000 exhibitors and vendors. The show's organizers help participants such as Henkel Harris, a Virginia-based manufacturer of high-end furniture, connect with buyers through directory listings, brochures, news releases, publicity events, multilingual marketing materials, seminars and networking events.   When the Market closes each spring and fall, Henkel Harris rightfully expects to leave with a notebook full of orders for what the firm's slogan claims is "Just Possibly America's Best Furniture."

Although tiny in scale compared to a trade show, a point-of-sale display can also be effective for heightening brand awareness, interest and excitement.   Marketers at Milka, which is owned by Kraft Foods and is the leading milk-chocolate brand in Europe, wanted a point-of-purchase display for airport retail shops.   The unit that was developed is a replica of the Milka cow – complete with lilac livery and a bell around its neck – whose shelves can store the brand's entire product range.   In addition to being functional, the display is so eye-catching it attracts travelers in airports around the world who might otherwise have overlooked the candy – or even the shop itself.   More store traffic for the retailer and more sales for Kraft mean both parties benefit.

Copyright permission Kraft Foods

Push also refers to sales promotions aimed at consumers, such as loyalty rewards, BOGOs (buy one, get one free offers), gifts with purchase, bonus sizes, rebates, sweepstakes, contests and retailer coupons (i.e., those distributed by stores, such as Safeway, rather than by manufacturers, such as Heinz).   In a social-networking-meets-discounting twist on coupons, social commerce companies Groupon (http://www.groupon.com/) and Living Social (http://www.livingsocial.com) publicize daily deals on behalf of firms that require a predetermined number of consumers to sign up in specified geographic markets before the discount will be offered.   For example, a Charlotte restaurant might sell a $20 gift card for $10 in an effort to increase patronage.   Consumers who want to take advantage of the offer have an incentive to encourage others to sign up for the deal so the minimum will be met.

In 2012, Canon won *Promo Magazine*'s top award for "Project Imagin8ion," a user-generated photo contest that inspired a short film created by Hollywood filmmaker Ron Howard.   The highly successful promotion garnered 100,000 submissions in three weeks http://www.chiefmarketer.com/pro-awards/2012-pro-award-winner-best-promotion-grey-alliance-for-canon-usa-14092012.

Pull strategies and tactics are targeted directly at end consumers and often have longer-run objectives related to increasing awareness, building preference, creating a brand image, repositioning a brand, or improving the brand's reputation, to name several. Examples of the elements of pull include:

- Advertising is a non-personal form of communication paid for by a sponsor and generally aimed at a mass audience with the intention of informing, educating, persuading or reminding them about a brand. Many people who hear the word "marketing" automatically think of advertising, even though it's actually just one part of promotion/integrated marketing communications – the fourth P.

  Advertisements can appear in expected places such as TV, radio and magazines, as well as in unexpected or unusual places, such as on airplane fuselages, urinals, airline tray tables, and even eggs.

  o Print: Magazine Publishers of America's Kelly Awards (to be relaunched in late 2013)
    http://www.magazine.org/insights-resources/magazine-advertising-case-studies/kelly-awards

  o Out-of-doors: Adzookie pays mortgages, gains neighborhood "billboards"

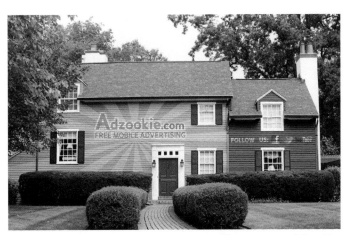

Photo courtesy Adzookie

  o Paid listings: Search "Internet banner ad" on Google and sponsored results appear at the top

- Broadcast

  - TV: Without using the actual tagline, Nike conveys the brand's "Just do it" mantra http://www.youtube.com/watch?v=n9yn_3fromg

  - Radio: Lose your license speeding, and you're "just a kid again" http://www.tfl.gov.uk/tfl/corporate/media/newscentre/young-drivers-radio-ad-speed.mp3

  - Internet: The Web Marketing Association selects winners of the Internet Advertising Competition http://www.iacaward.org/iac/winners.asp

- Public relations: McDonald's celebrates African-American culture 365 days a year http://www.365black.com/365black/whatis.jsp

- Cause-related co-promotion: Lilly Pulitzer teams up with Nabisco's Animal Crackers to benefit the Urban Arts Partnership http://blog.lillypulitzer.com/2011/04/15/barnums-animals-and-lilly-pulitzer-team-up-again/

Photo courtesy Lilly Pulitzer

- Sponsorship: JPMorgan Chase has sponsored the U.S. Open Tennis Championships for more than 30 years http://2012.usopen.org/en_US/about/sponsors_jpmorgan.html

- Manufacturer coupons (in the package, on the package, at checkout, online, in the mail, in a newspaper supplement, on a cell phone)

- Mobile marketing: Dos Equis engages audiences with a16-city "Most Interesting Show in the World" tour http://www.youtube.com/watch?v=gGnYK_u1C38

- Product placement: Alec Baldwin and Tina Fey openly promote Verizon on 30 Rock http://www.youtube.com/watch?v=d36wUmJGzvA

- Viral marketing: The video of Red Bull's Stratos jump had more than 171 million total views http://www.youtube.com/watch?v=Dt0QuBsGU20

- Logoed merchandise: Imprinted pens offer continuing visibility for the brand

- Publicity: Dawn Saves Wildlife Campaign helps birds and marine mammals http://www.dawn-dish.com/en_US/savingwildlife/home.do

- Events: Milwaukee Great Circus Parade is part of a four-day festival http://circusworld.wisconsinhistory.org/Parade/EventOverview.aspx

- Blogs: Flickr online photo management has a companion site http://blog.flickr.net/en

- Web sites: Visitors can watch videos, post comments and buy KiD CuDi music, apparel and other gear http://www.kidcudi.com/

- Mobile phone messaging: ESPN allows fans to sign up for news, score and event alerts http://proxy.espn.go.com/mobile/alerts/signup

- Direct mail: Valpak delivers 20 billion offers annually in 490 million envelopes sent to 42 million U.S. and Canadian addresses http://www.valpak.com/coupons/home

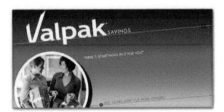

Photo courtesy Valpak

- Advergaming: Fans are willing to pay for M&M's Brand Chocolate Factory advergame http://www.ecommercetimes.com/story/76841.html

- Social media: French car maker Peugeot's Panama unit recently ran a contest rewarding fans for completing a Pinterest puzzle. To get pieces missing from the puzzle, fans had to go to Peugeot Panama's Facebook Page or website http://pinterest.com/peugeotofficial/

- Buzz/word-of-mouth: In what is considered one of the most creative and successful publicity events ever, Taco Bell would have given a free taco to every American if the Soviet Mir space station had hit a 40-square-foot target floating in the Pacific Ocean http://www.spaceref.com/news/viewpr.html?pid=4152

- And, of course, *etc.*: Green Pharmaceuticals paid $37,000 in an eBay auction to put the logo for its SnoreStop brand on the forehead of college student Andrew Fischer.

Photo courtesy SnoreStop

The changing communications environment requires marketers to search for new and different ways of capturing and keeping customers' attention. Mashable, an online digital news source (http://mashable.com/), sponsored a Fast Pitch competition in 2010 for start-up companies that develop innovative ways to enhance engagement between brands and their customers. The winner was Foodspotting, http://www.foodspotting.com/#/, which provides photos of more than 65,000 foods and locations where they can be found, uploaded by more than 105,000 users.

Word-of-mouth communication
The cacophony of messages, fragmentation of media into increasingly specialized niches, and general consumer disinterest and distrust make mass communications far less effective than it used to be. Individuals in the U.S. are exposed to anywhere from 300 to 3,000 marketing stimuli a day related to existing brands or to the 20,000 – 40,000 new products introduced every year. Their (our!) response to this confusing clutter is to zip, zap, toss away, turn off and tune out.

As overall viewership and readership figures for TV, radio and print media have declined, so, too, have the relative roles of these and other conventional media in many firms' marketing communications programs. Word-of-mouth communications – consumer-to-consumer conversation, rather than marketer-to-consumer information – is sometimes far more effective than traditional advertising. The more a brand is talked about positively in public, the more credibility it gains. Hence, nowadays a company must motivate customers to talk to one another about its brand, rather than focus exclusively on inducing customers to listen to its marketing messages.

How do you build word of mouth? By doing something worth talking about!

A 10-person Brussels advertising agency, So Nice, was having a problem with clients paying their bills later and later. So it sent them an email announcing a staff cut and asking them to choose which employee should go by following a link to a Web site, where the prospective terminated employees list their strengths and weaknesses. The email also garnered an interested reaction outside the company's client base. In five days, the site had 30,000 unique visitors casting 17,500 votes.

Because of their brand's association with turkey and Thanksgiving, Kraft Foods placed Stove Top posters in 50 Chicago bus shelters and on the holiday passed out samples of its new Quick Cups stuffing to passengers and passersby. Ten of the shelters were fitted with ceiling-mounted heaters that pumped out warm air and featured "Cold Provided by Winter. Warmth Provided by Us." posters. The value of the media coverage the idea received and the buzz it generated far exceeded the company's $100,000 installation cost.

The most revolutionary change in marketing communications has been due to the rise of social media (e.g., Facebook, YouTube, Pinterest and Twitter), which are technology-based tools – primarily Internet and mobile – for sharing conversations, communications and information among individuals.

Socialnomics (http://www.socialnomics.net/), an online analytics site, has produced a Social Revolution 2013 video (http://www.youtube.com/watch?v=QUCfFcchw1w) full of facts, statistics and information about the impact of social networking on people and business. According to the video, accessing social media sites is the #1 activity on the Internet; 93 percent of companies use social media; 53 percent of all tweets mentions brands; two people join LinkedIn every second (http://www.linkedin.com/); and the Ford Explorer launch of Facebook got more views than a Super Bowl ad.

A 2010 ROI Research study of 3,000 social network users revealed that 37 percent learned about new product/services from a social networking site, 32 percent recommended a product, service or brand to friends via a social networking site, 32 percent of those who use Twitter re-tweet content provided by a firm, and 50 percent of Facebook users click on the site's ads to "Like" a brand. Almost six in 10 online shoppers say customer reviews affect their buying behavior, according to "The 2011 Social Shopping Study" by PowerReviews http://www.powerreviews.com/assets/download/Social_Shopping_2011_Brief1.pdf.

To determine a brand's Web visibility, marketers can check How Sociable http://www.howsociable.com/; Brand Buzz Index http://www.brandbuzzindex.com/; BrandIndex, which identifies Ford, Amazon, Subway, History Channel, Lowe's, V8, Walgreen's, YouTube, Kindle and Cheerios as the top most buzzed-about brands in the first six months of 2013 (http://www.brandindex.com/ranking/us/2013-mid/top-buzz-rankings); Topsy http://topsy.com/; Google Analytics http://www.google.com/analytics/; Facebook Insights https://www.facebook.com/insights/; and Twitter https://twitter.com/.

YouTube, which is owned by Google, has proven to be an important and effective social media channel for many brands. One of the best examples of a successful marketing communications video campaign is the "Will It Blend" series created by Blendtec. The videos show CEO Tom Dickson "pureeing" hockey pucks, golf clubs and cell phones in the company's powerful blender. The Will It Blend – Crowbar video alone, http://www.youtube.com/watch?v=ifzdez7FRbk, has had more than 4.9 million hits. The company says the campaign led to a five-fold increase in sales.

Even paper towels have been the subject of successful YouTube campaigns. In August 2010, Procter & Gamble announced that the latest music video from Bounty had garnered a cumulative audience of 650,000 in less than two weeks, with 450,000 views on the first day alone http://www.youtube.com/watch?v=X2wMRH7hbfk.. "White Glove" features hip-hop legend Joseph "Rev Run" Simmons of Run-DMC fame as Principal Simmons and builds off the success of the brand's "Bring It" video, which achieved more than one million views http://www.youtube.com/watch?v=ry6H0HcZVlA.

Wikipedia lists more than 150 individuals or groups who became brand personalities as a result of YouTube http://en.wikipedia.org/wiki/List_of_YouTube_personalities. The list includes Justin Bieber, whose "Baby" music video has 700 million views http://www.youtube.com/charts/videos_views?t=a

Just a few months earlier, Visible Measures, an agency that compiles Internet video and viral marketing metrics (http://www.visiblemeasures.com/), reported that Lady Gaga had become the first artist to reach one billion online video views, primarily on YouTube and Vevo, (http://www.vevo.com/), a music video joint venture between Google and Universal Music Group, Sony Music and Abu Dhabi Media. She had 65 videos that each had 100 million views or more.

YouTube can also be used to spread damaging information about a brand. United Breaks Guitars tells the story of Dave Carroll, a musician and United Airlines passenger who watched helplessly as baggage handlers broke his instrument by literally throwing it onto a conveyor belt. His video has had more than 8.7 million hits http://www.youtube.com/watch?v=5YGc4zOqozo.

Social Twist, http://tellafriend.socialtwist.com/, has a free Tell-a-Friend (TAF) widget that allows users to forward marketing messages with one click to their social circle. The customizable widget is displayed as a Web page pop-up that links to more than 80 different services for content distribution. The premium version for brands comes pre-loaded with analytics to monitor viral campaigns. Since the service launched in 2008, the widget has delivered more than four billion impressions through more than 70,000 Web sites.

What makes social media so unusual and important is their emphasis on consumer-generated content that is not, and cannot be, controlled by marketers. When a Penn State marketing professor and his colleagues studied the content of half-a-million tweets, they found that 20 percent mentioned brands.

Not all brand mentions are positive. In 2008, Johnson & Johnson pulled its "Motrin Mom" campaign after mothers created outraged tweets about what they saw as the ad's implication that children were fashion accessories.

Twitter can be accessed through more than 50,000 third-party Internet and mobile applications. In 2012, more than 175 million tweets a day were being sent. As a result of the service's pervasive use, companies are jumping on the Twitter bandwagon, too. Zappos, an online retailer, uses Twitter to build a helpful, trustworthy, friendly image for the brand. "Wow, Zappos got an order from a customer shipping to McMurdo Station in Antarctica!" is an excited tweet sent by one of the company's employees, most who have active accounts.

Google Real-Time https://support.google.com/analytics/answer/1638635?hl=en, allows users to search for tweets and other social updates, news articles and blog posts. At http://www.browsys.com/, users can search Twitter, blogs, YouTube and SlideShare, as well as Google and Bing.

Facebook is even more popular than Twitter. As of May 2013, the social networking site had more than 42 million pages, with 1.1 billion active users worldwide – 665 million of whom log in daily for an average of 20 minutes. Every 60 seconds, 510 comments are posted, 293,000 statuses are updated, and 136,000 photos are uploaded (http://zephoria.com/social-media/top-15-valuable-facebook-statistics/).

Companies have tapped into the site's popularity by developing pages that allow them to connect to and engage with "fans," who visit to watch videos, download music, learn about promotions, interact with other customers, blog, and participate in a variety of other activities designed to increase their connectedness to the brand. For example, the Mtn Dew page rallies one million fans into action to pick flavors, colors, names, packaging designs, and advertising for new varieties. Lady Gaga set a record in June 2010 for acquiring 10 million "Likes", surpassing President Obama's mark by 700,000.

In July 2013, Inside Facebook identified Facebook for Every Phone as the most liked Facebook page with more than 263 million fans. Singer Rihanna was the most popular person on Facebook, trailed closely by rapper Eminem. The most popular game page was Zynga's Texas HoldEm Poker. The only non-Internet or non-entertainment brand on the list of the top 25 was Coca-Cola in the eighth spot (http://www.insidefacebook.com/2013/07/03/top-25-facebook-pages-july-2013/)

In August 2010 *Forbes* and a panel of marketing experts ranked the 20 best social media campaigns of all time based on overall success and the quality and creativity of the execution. The top spot went to one of the first-ever viral marketing efforts, for the 1999 movie *The Blair Witch Project* http://www.forbes.com/2010/08/17/facebook-old-spice-farmville-pepsi-forbes-viral-marketing-cmo-network-social-media_slide.html.

Not all products/services or brands enjoy high "talkability" ratings. But those more boring than, say, an iPhone, can borrow relevance from consumer interests, problems or issues. American Express created the Members' Project to choose deserving charities https://www.facebook.com/membersproject. Procter & Gamble knew girls discuss music, cliques, and school, but not tampons, so the firm created http://www.beinggirl.co.uk/home.php as a vehicle for delivering feminine care information.

According to Steve Hall of AdRants, a marketing and advertising commentary site, successful social media campaigns are authentic, make it "brainlessly easy" for people to participate, include a clear and concise call to action, and avoid blatant self-promotion, among other characteristics http://www.adrants.com/2010/10/seven-traits-of-successful-social-media.php.

Marketers can monitor and measure consumer sentiment toward a brand using a technology known as text analytics, which is software that extracts insights from social media sites, databases, news articles, and internal documents. According to Forrester Research, the market for text analytics will rise to almost $1 billion in 2014 from $499 million in 2011.

Malcom Gladwell, author of *The Tipping Point*, identifies three factors that help ideas capture public interest and reach the critical mass necessary to fuel a social epidemic. First is The Law of the Few, which suggests that a company focus on three types of people who create the epidemic – mavens, who are extremely knowledgeable about an area or subject; connectors, who know a huge number of other people; and salesmen, who possess terrific persuasive powers.

Yappem, http://www.yappem.com/index.html, gives users a chance to earn gift cards by posting about interactions with brands and businesses. Each shared brand experience is worth coins, which can be exchanged for gift cards to major retailers. Empire Avenue, http://empireavenue.com/, is an online influence stock exchange combined with an ad platform that allows members to convert their reach and influence into revenue.

Gladwell's second factor is Stickiness, which necessitates that the idea be expressed in a way that is memorable and that motivates people to act. Brothers Chip and Dan Heath, authors of *Made to Stick*, say sticky ideas are those that are easily understood and remembered, and that change opinions, behaviors, or values. They identify key principles of stickiness: simplicity, unexpectedness, concreteness, credibility, emotion, and stories.

Gladwell's final factor is The Power of Context, which requires that those spreading the idea be able to organize groups and communities around it. Gaia Online http://www.gaiaonline.com/ is a community of 23 million mostly teenage users who talk about anime and video games. WeeWorld, http://www.weeworld.com//, a virtual world for teens, is another of the more than 200 online social network sites identified by Wikipedia http://en.wikipedia.org/wiki/List_of_social_networking_websites.

Who are the brand's most engaged customers, the ones with the highest likelihood of generating word-of-mouth? "White high school teenagers" isn't an answer. "High school teens who strive to dress, act and think differently from the norm" might be. Finding out what makes a brand's influential customers tick is the key to finding out what will make them talk!

Keep in mind, however, that regardless of its pervasiveness and popularity, no single media – social or traditional – can by itself achieve a company's marketing objectives. The overarching goal is to build a level of engagement with consumers that fosters the creation, maintenance and enhancement of mutually beneficial relationships. Achieving success in that regard requires a mix of complementary elements integrated into a synergistic whole that delivers maximum impact within the intended target market.

Whew! And just how is that done? Ask the Marines; they seem to know! As detailed earlier, the Corps' campaign results exceeded recruiting goals and met or surpassed objectives related to the target market's attitudes, beliefs, and perceptions.

Knowing what you're trying to achieve is the first step. Yogi Berra said, "If you don't know where you're going, you'll probably end up somewhere else." Once the destination is known, figuring out the route is much more straightforward. That's as true in integrated marketing communications as it is in life!

Appendix
Financial aspects of marketing:
terminology and formulas

The saying, "It takes money to make money," might well have been coined by a marketer!

The activities associated with creating value for a firm's customers aren't costless, or even inexpensive. Conducting market and consumer research, designing and developing exceptional products and services, generating and implementing successful marketing strategies, formulating and executing persuasive integrated marketing communications, establishing effective channel systems, enhancing customer service, improving production or service operations, and making the countless continuing investments required to create, maintain and improve mutually beneficial relationships with customers can consume substantial financial resources.

Like all sound investments, however, marketing expenditures can return huge dividends in the form reliable streams of revenue from happy customers, who show their gratitude by delivering the dollars needed to keep the business in business.

Because marketing is a user and producer of capital on a significant scale, it's imperative that marketers be familiar with rudimentary fiscal concepts relevant to the field. A basic understanding of such concepts is essential to responsible decision-making.

As you read through what follows, think about how each of the terms would apply to your lemonade stand or to some other product, service or situation that aids your comprehension.

Selling price – the sum of money at which a company offers a product/service to its customers; composed of two parts: cost of goods sold per unit and margin per unit

Selling price per unit = Cost of goods sold per unit + margin per unit

- The manufacturer's selling price – abbreviated *MSP* – is the price at which the producer sells to retailers. For example, McNeil Consumer Healthcare Division sells Benadryl to food, drug and mass merchandise retail stores, who then sell the over-the-counter allergy medication to consumers.

- The retailer's selling price – abbreviated *RSP* – is the price at which the retailer sells to final consumers. For example, CVS buys from McNeil and sells to individuals who suffer from hay fever.

- In some cases, the manufacturer is also a retailer. For example, Apple sells not only to Walmart, but also directly to consumers. In such cases, the price at which the manufacturer sells to a retailer – the MSP – is lower than the price at which the manufacturer sells to end consumers – the RSP. In other words, Walmart pays less to buy from Apple than you or I pay!

Cost of goods sold (COGS) – the expense associated with producing (or acquiring) a product/service offered to customers; usually expressed on a per-unit or percentage basis, i.e., COGS per unit or % COGS per unit; often referred to as variable cost because the total changes as the number of units produced (or acquired) changes

$$\% \text{ COGS} = \text{COGS per unit/Selling price per unit}$$

$$\text{Total COGS} = \text{COGS per unit} \times \text{\# of units produced (or acquired)}$$

- The manufacturer's selling price, MSP, is the retailer's cost of goods sold, COGS

Margin – the arithmetic difference between the cost of producing (or acquiring) a product/service and its selling price; can be expressed in dollars/cents or percentages

$$\text{Margin} = \text{Selling price} - \text{COGS}$$

$$\% \text{ margin} = (\text{Selling price} - \text{COGS})/ \text{ Selling price}$$

- % margin is the percentage of selling price that's "left over" after the firm covers its costs

$$100\% - \% \text{ margin} = \% \text{ COGS}$$

- Margin is not the same as "markup," which is a term used only by retailers, not by manufacturers

$$\text{Markup} = (\text{selling price} - \text{COGS})/\text{COGS}$$

  o Because the denominator is smaller in a markup than in a margin calculation (i.e., COGS versus selling price), markup is always larger than margin

Unit sales – the total number of units sold in a given period

Revenue – the total dollar amount of sales in a given period; the company's "top line"

$$\text{Total revenue} = \text{Selling price per unit} \times \text{\# of units sold}$$

Fixed costs – expenses that do not vary with or depend on the level of production or output, such as rent or salary or marketing budget or research and development costs

- The amount of money budgeted for marketing is the primary fixed cost you'll encounter in this course

Total costs – the sum of fixed and total variable costs

Total costs = Fixed costs + (COGS per unit x # of units)

Profit – the arithmetic difference between total revenue and total costs; the "bottom line"

Profit = Total revenue – total costs

= Total revenue – (Fixed costs + Total variable costs)

Break-even point – the point at which a company neither makes a profit nor loses money; the point at which a company just covers or recoups its total costs (or expenditures or investment); the point at which total revenue = total costs (or expenditures or investment) and, consequently, total profit = $0; can be expressed in dollars or units

At the break-event point:

Profit = $0

$0 = Total revenue – total costs

Total revenue = Total costs

(Selling price/unit x # units) = Fixed costs + total variable costs

Fixed costs = (Selling price/unit x # units) – total variable costs

Fixed costs = (Selling price/unit x # units) – (variable cost/unit x # units)

Fixed costs = (Selling price/unit – variable cost/unit) x # units

Fixed costs = $ margin/unit x # units

Break-even point in # units = Fixed costs/$ margin per unit

Break-even point in $ = Fixed costs/% margin

- Note that only two pieces of information are required in order to perform a break-even calculation: 1.) the total amount of money spent/budgeted that the firm wants to recoup, i.e., the "fixed cost," and 2.) the margin, in dollars or percent.

- The break-even point is used in marketing to determine the total sales – in units or dollars – required to pay for a plan, program or promotion

    o For example, suppose a company is thinking of boosting its advertising budget $5 million in an effort to increase a brand's sales. Before allocating the funds, marketers should determine how many additional units or dollars of the brand must be sold in order to cover the extra amount. It makes no sense to spend more money to stimulate sales if it leads to an overall financial loss.

        - If the margin were 100%, then the firm would need to sell an additional $5 million in order to break even on the spending increase ($5 million/100%). But because part of the selling price must be used to cover the brand's COGS, the firm must actually sell more than the amount of the increase.

Market share – the percentage of total sales in a product/service category (or industry) captured by a particular brand (or company); can be expressed as a percentage of total dollars or units in a category (e.g., canned dog food) or industry (e.g., dog food or pet food, whichever is relevant)

Brand's $ market share = Brand's $ sales/Total $ sales volume in category

Brand's unit market share = Brand's unit sales/Total unit sales volume in category

Company's $ market share = Company's $ sales/Total $ sales volume in industry

Company's unit market share = Company's unit sales/Total unit sales volume in industry

Break-even market share – the market share required for a firm to break even on an expenditure; puts the break-even point "in perspective," i.e., provides a frame of reference for evaluating the likelihood that the break-even point will be attained

- A break-event point of 750 million allergy pills sounds like an impossible amount, but if the total market size is 12 billion, then the break-even market share is only 6.25%

    - 750mm/12b = .0625 = 6.25%

Time to break even – the amount of time required for a firm to break even on an expenditure; puts the break-even point "in perspective," i.e., provides a frame of reference for evaluating the likelihood that the break-even point will be attained

- A break-even point of $300 million sounds like a huge amount, but if a company's annual sales are $1.8 billion, then the time to break even is only .17 years, or two months

  - $300mm/$1.8b per year = .17 years
  - .17 years x 12 months per year = 2 months

Income statement/pro forma income statement – the financial document that shows how much a company made or lost, or expects to make or lose, during a particular period of time. Often referred to as a *P&L*, or a profit and loss statement. The income statement begins with sales revenue and, ultimately, ends with net income (also referred to as profit or earnings).

Typically, an income statement is backward-looking in that it shows actual performance during a time period of interest. For example, a statement can cover last quarter, the last three quarters, last year, or even the last "x" number of years.

In some cases, however, a company wants to look ahead at the potential economic consequences of a business decision or transaction. In the marketing arena, many strategies are aimed at boosting sales revenue, which often necessitates increased investment. The additional funds can be spent on the product/service itself, on distribution, and/or on promotion. Before making a go/no-go decision regarding a planned marketing expenditure, management would of course want to know what the overall financial impact might be. In such cases, the marketing department would prepare a *pro forma* income statement (more simply referred to as a *pro forma*), which predicts future performance based on expectations, or forecasts, of sales, costs, expenses and profit.

Depending on the accounting approach used to prepare them, income statements/pro formas can differ in terms of the number and types of components included. For the purposes of this course, we'll generally use a simple template that focuses on the elements most relevant to marketing: sales revenue, cost of goods sold, gross profit, marketing expenses, and net income.

On the next page is an example of a two-year pro forma for a fictional food company planning to launch a new dessert pizza. Notations to the right of numbers are for explanatory purposes only; they wouldn't appear on a real document.

Notice important features of the statement:

1. The figures for the two years are displayed side-by-side, to enhance comparability
2. Dollar signs are included (of course, it's about money!)
3. All decimal points line up and commas are appropriately placed, both of which improve readability
4. Cents have been eliminated; when the numbers are big, round up or down

Sweet-za Dessert Pizza
Two-year launch
Pro forma income statement

	Year 1	Year 2	
Units sold	5,194,860	7,127,645	(Volume model forecast)
Sales revenue	$45,143,333	$61,939,235	($8.69/unit MSP x units)
Cost of goods sold	$15,800,167	$21,678,732	(35% assumed COGS)
Gross profit	$29,343,166	$40,260,503	(Revenue – COGS)
Marketing			
Slotting allowances	$ 2,750,000		
Trade promotions	$ 325,000		
Sampling	$ 225,000		
Awareness building	$28,700,000	$22,000,000	
Total	$32,000,000	$22,000,000	(Annual launch budget)
Net income	($ 2,656,834)	$18,260,503	(It is standard to double underline net income, and to signify a loss by enclosing the number in parentheses)

You can always compute the percentage margin and the percentage cost of goods sold from the income statement.

% Margin = (Sales revenue – Cost of goods sold)/Sales revenue

~ or ~

% Margin = Gross profit/Sales revenue

~ and ~

% Cost of goods sold = Cost of goods sold/Sales revenue

Of course, as noted previously, the % Cost of goods sold = 100% – % Margin

CPSIA information can be obtained
at www.ICGtesting.com
Printed in the USA
LVIC06n1157020514
384124LV00006B/12

* 9 7 8 0 9 8 3 4 1 5 7 2 5 *